STRANGE HEAVEN

Strange Heaven

The Virgin Mary
as Woman, Mother, Disciple, and Advocate

JON M. SWEENEY

PARACLETE PRESS
BREWSTER, MASSACHUSETTS

Strange Heaven: The Virgin Mary as Woman,
Mother, Disciple, and Advocate

2006   First Printing

ISBN 1-55725-432-X

Library of Congress Cataloging-in-Publication Data
Sweeney, Jon M., 1967–
Strange heaven : the Virgin Mary as woman, mother, disciple, and advocate / Jon M. Sweeney.
p. cm.
Includes index.
ISBN 1-55725-432-X
1. Mary, Blessed Virgin, Saint. I. Title.
BT603.S94 2006
232.91—dc22   2006011943

Published by Paraclete Press
Brewster, Massachusetts
www.paracletepress.com

10 9 8 7 6 5 4 3 2 1

Printed in the United States of America

In memory of
M. Basil Pennington, OCSO

† June 3, 2005

At life's last moment fleeting;
your Son for us entreating,
O Virgin Mother, grant that we,
with you, may Christ embrace.

CONTENTS

Strange Heaven

Contents

For *that faire blessed Mother-maid,*
Whose flesh redeem'd us . . .
Whose wombe was a strange heav'n, for there
God cloath'd himselfe, and grew,
Our zealous thankes wee poure.
As her deeds were
Our helpes, so are her prayers . . .

—John Donne, from "The Virgin Mary,"
part V of *A Litanie*

INTRODUCTION
Imagining Mary

E KNOW ALMOST NOTHING ABOUT HER for certain. There are no surviving documents that were written in her own hand. No letters, no diaries. There are relics, of course—thousands upon thousands of relics. One sparsely written inventory prepared in 1346 for a French chapel includes: "Item, the hairs of St. Mary; item, from her robe; item, a shallow ivory box without any ornament save only a knob of copper, which box contains some of the flower which the Blessed Virgin held before her Son, and of the window through which the Archangel Gabriel entered when he saluted her."[1] We also don't have any teachings of Mary. Erasmus once complained—"We kiss the shoes of the saints and their dirty handkerchiefs and we leave their books, their most holy and efficacious relics, neglected"—but in Mary's case, there are no books, either.

There are also no images of her that can be dated to first-century Palestine. We have her likeness, however, which is supposed to have been handed down generation to generation since St. Luke first painted it. The tradition of Luke as Mary's first iconographer probably began because it is mostly his Gospel that preserves what we *do* know about her from the New Testament. Medieval Christians believed that Luke actually interviewed Mary for the writing of his text. As he explains at the outset of his Gospel: "[These events] were handed on to us by those who from the beginning were eyewitnesses and servants of the world." For whatever reason, Luke seems to have understood Mary and her perspective. This is likely why there are many icons depicting Luke painting an icon of the Virgin. Although not exact physical images of Mary, Catholic and Orthodox Christians usually believe that these icons present the spirit of Mary, and offer a window to her in heaven.

We also don't have eyewitness accounts of her life. Mary would have been in her mid to late forties at the time of Jesus' passion, resurrection, and ascension. Contrary to the legend of Luke's friendship with her, most scholars agree that the first of the New Testament Gospels was written no sooner than twenty-five years after those events had occurred; Mary would most likely have been gone by then.

We never seem to imagine that Mary could have constructed her own image. Surely it is possible that, like many saints that came after her, Mary deliberately created and nurtured the images of her sanctity that have been handed down to us since the days of the early church. Instead, we usually presume that Mary's image was built for her—an idealized portrait that then says far more about us than it does about her.

The dominant image of Mary that we inherited from the ancient church is of her as a refined, graceful, pensive young woman who was nevertheless full of wisdom. She was also seen as quickly subservient to the will of a masculine God, his angels, and the husband who was appointed to care for her. In the eyes of the ancients, Mary became what feminist scholars would today call the first of the *domesticated goddesses*—which is not intended to be a compliment to her, or to us. An imposed super-femininity emasculated her strength and wisdom.

These qualities of the idealized Virgin became spiritual ideals for centuries of Christian women and men. One example of how they seeped completely into our culture comes from the stories of Protestant author Harriet Beecher Stowe; she wrote about Mary in two of her novels that came after *Uncle Tom's Cabin*. To imbibe the lesson of Mary, according to Stowe, is to discover "women's eternal power of self-sacrifice to what she deems noblest." In *Agnes of Sorrento* (1862), Stowe describes her Virgin Mary-character, Agnes, using language that could be taken directly from a medieval chronicle of the Virgin:

> She might have been fifteen or thereabouts, but was so small of stature that she seemed yet a child. Her black hair was parted in a white unbroken seam down to the high forehead, whose serious arch, like that of a cathedral door, spoke of thought and prayer. Beneath the shadows of this brow lay brown, translucent eyes, into whose thoughtful depths one might look as pilgrims gaze into the waters of some saintly well, cool and pure down to the unblemished sand at the bottom. The small lips had a gentle compression, which indicated a repressed strength of feeling; while the straight line of the nose, and the flexible, delicate nostril, were perfect as in those sculptured fragments of the antique which the soil of Italy so often gives forth to the day from the

3

sepulchers of the past. The habitual pose of the head and face had the shy uplooking grace of a violet; and yet there was a grave tranquility of expression, which gave a peculiar degree of character to the whole figure.

At the moment at which we have called your attention, the fair head is bent, the long eyelashes lie softly down on the pale, smooth cheek; for the Ave Maria bell is sounding from the Cathedral of Sorrento, and the child is busy with her beads.

"The child is busy with her beads." In other words, she is praying the rosary, entreating Mary, the intercessor to Christ. The Virgin Mary is, in fact, often pictured in religious art holding rosary beads, as the originator of the practice now devoted to her, and the messages of Mary in many of her apparitions have been to pray the rosary, or, at least, to pray.

One sentence from Luke's Gospel says volumes about this young woman: "Mary kept all these things, pondering them in her heart" (2:19 RSV). Such a statement does not mean that she simply thought about heavenly things; it says something, too, about her wisdom. She was not a quick or careless thinker. Bernardino of Siena takes this notion a bit deeper; in a famous sermon delivered on August 15, 1427, Bernardino spent two hours relaying to his audience what he called the twelve qualities of the Virgin Mary. Number one was her intelligence. Despite our inherited images of Mary as a servant of a masculine God, hers was not a credulous faith.

Thanks to scholarly developments, in recent decades we have come closer than ever to knowing the historical person, Mary of Nazareth. Archaeology, sociology, and historical investigations into first-century Judaism and the role of women have helped us to paint a picture of who she might have been. There is Mary (or Miriam, as she would have been called in Hebrew) the Mother of God, the object of devotion and the subject of numerous minutiae of Roman Catholic theology, but there is also Mary, the simple woman who became the mother of Jesus. By all of the earliest accounts, she was unmarried and pregnant, poor and insignificant, a woman living in an occupied country. One recent biographical description of her goes like this:

> She is thirteen. Short and wiry, with dark olive skin. The trace of a mustache on her upper lip, soft black down on her arms and legs. The muscles are hard knots in her arms, solid lines in her calves. Her hair is almost black, and has been folded into a single braid down her back for as long as she can remember. The weight of it raises her chin and makes her walk tall, as she has learned to do when carrying jars of water or bundles of kindling on her head. You don't bend under the burden. You root into the ground and grow out of it, reaching up and becoming taller. The greater the weight, the taller you become: the peasant woman's secret of making the burden light.[2]

But most of what fascinates us about Mary is not reducible to historical fact or theory. It is her *myth* that draws us: Her power to fascinate us intellectually is surpassed only by her ability to inspire devotion.

Dietrich Bonhoeffer once wrote to a friend, "I must learn more about the Middle Ages. We need them." Bonhoeffer understood that the medieval period was a time when religion, culture, and spirituality blended almost seamlessly. God seemed to most people, then, to be alive and active in the world. People of all backgrounds and economic classes shared a sacramental view of the world around them: The creation was alive with spiritual meaning; God was among them, and there was no aspect of life that stood outside of divine influence and spirit. Also, humans were God's special project, formed by hand out of earth at the beginning of time. Like a potter, God built humans carefully, and the notion of a perfect, idealized creation still seemed possible. In the chapters that follow, we will often turn to the imagination of the Middle Ages in order to discover the traditions and beliefs that have surrounded the Virgin for ages. The feelings and actions of the devout toward Mary today are a mirror image of those of our medieval ancestors. Despite enlightenments, science, and other notions of progress, so many of us still bow our heads, finger our beads, and listen for her comfort and assurance.

What is it that motivates twenty-first century Christians, modern in every other respect, to bow like medieval pilgrims before statues of the Virgin Mary in churches around the world, praying earnestly for her inter-cession before God? Also, why would an icon of the Virgin

Introduction

be one of a pope's most cherished possessions, hanging above his private desk in the Vatican, "watching over my daily service to the church," as John Paul II once explained during a homily? That icon is called the Madonna of Kazan, named for a city about five hundred miles east of Moscow in the Republic of Tatarstan. When a papal delegation traveled to the former Soviet Union in order to return it to the patriarchs of the Russian Orthodox Church at the end of August 2004, why did that gesture become one of the most important signs of improving ecumenical relations between the two churches in recent memory?[3] Exploring these questions is a way of getting to the heart of why Mary matters.

At the same time, why does Mary also sometimes spark violent reactions against religion, or her, or God? Images of Mary can lead to sudden feelings and emotions from people, even those who may not be religious. Many times I have seen tears on the faces of people in the halls of art galleries, where most observations of religious art are so cool and detached. In other instances, an image of Mary can cause the mentally unstable to come unhinged, as, for instance, when in 1972 a man in New York City climbed onto Michelangelo's *Pietà* (which was on loan from the Vatican) and began pounding Mary with a hammer. He hit her in the face, breaking part of an eye, and he severed a finger on the famous left hand of the Virgin—the hand that is tilted up as if to say, "I accept what must happen to my son." Similarly, *The Virgin and the Child with Saint Anne and Saint John the Baptist* appears to be the most vandalized painting in London's National Gallery, having twice been damaged. In 1962, it was attacked with a bottle of ink, and in 1987, with a sawed-off shotgun.

She has had the power to rouse armies and to rally great causes. Images of Mary were once carried proudly before Russian, Greek, Spanish, and Italian armies as they marched into battle. The ancient Israelites followed the Ark of the Covenant and the French and the Ethiopians the cross, but many other armies enlisted the Virgin Mary as some sort of divine protection from worldly harm. The Spanish conquistadors, in fact, frequently employed images of Mary on this continent in their battles for Mexico, and her likeness became synonymous with dominance and victory. How could the Blessed Virgin's image be honored as *La Conquistadora?*

Mary has become a symbol of national identity. She is the patron saint of Cuba, revered as the Virgin of Charity. She is the patron of Poland, in the enigmatic figure of the Black Madonna, Our Lady of Czestochowa. She has even rallied labor unions. Why did Cesar Chavez feel that devotion to the Virgin was essential to the public fight for justice for California's Mexican farm workers?

Over the centuries, Catholic and Orthodox Christians have imagined roles such as these for Mary out of their expansive and sacramental ways of viewing the world around them. In the sixteenth century, Protestants moved swiftly in their attempt to cut off this imagining, but they didn't account for the more subtle means by which the ancient ways of knowing may stick with us. It is natural, now, to want to turn back and look at what we have left behind.

The Catholic imagination is powerful, in ways that the Protestant imagination cannot match. When the Protestant imagination focuses on the gulf that separates us from God, the Catholic imagination sees the sacramental nature of all that is around us. While Protestant spirituality focuses on the Word of God (preaching it, hearing it, applying it) in order to repair the separation that divides us from God, Catholic spirituality focuses on finding, lifting, and releasing the Spirit of God that is sometimes hidden or latent in the world around us.

Introduction

Catholic priest and novelist Andrew Greeley explains: "Catholics live in an enchanted world, a world of statues and holy water, stained glass and votive candles, saints and religious medals, rosary beads and holy pictures. But these Catholic paraphernalia are mere hints of a deeper and more pervasive religious sensibility which inclines Catholics to see the Holy lurking in creation. As Catholics, we find our houses and our world haunted by a sense that the objects, events, and persons of daily life are revelations of grace."[4]

Archetypes of our ancient, religious imagination—inherited from generations of our ancestors—are always with us, bubbling beneath the surface of our conscious selves. The motherhood of God is one of these archetypes, an idea that is common in many religious traditions, as is sainthood, or the possible culmination of the divine and the earthly within us. Both of these archetypes are central to understanding why images and legends of the Virgin Mary, if not dogma about her, still draw us today. In other words, we don't always "decide" to turn our attention to Mary. It may even be somehow hard-wired into us. As Rowan Williams, the archbishop of Canterbury, recently said, Mary "stands for the making strange of what is familiar and the homeliness of what is strange."[5]

The central act of Mary's life was one in which she was also acted upon by God. Did she have the option to say no? We'll never know for sure. But she didn't say no, and her womb became a "strange heaven," in the words of poet John Donne. This description perhaps best summarizes the feeling that many people, all of us onlookers, have toward Mary's life and vocation. It was strange indeed.

PART ONE

Mary in the Bible

[SOPHIA, OR WISDOM] is a reflection of eternal light, a spotless mirror of the working of God, and an image of his goodness. Although she is but one, she can do all things, and while remaining in herself, she renews all things; in every generation she passes into holy souls and makes them friends of God, and prophets. . . . She is more beautiful than the sun, and excels every constellation of the stars.

—Wisdom of Solomon, 7:26–29 (from the apocrypha)

Why a Virgin?

SHE IS HISTORY'S GREATEST EMBLEM OF PURITY—
a fitting place for God to be born. In ancient civ-
ilizations, there was no greater symbol for a
woman than her virginal purity. Given the prevalence of
rape, arranged marriage, incest and other factors, virginity
was very difficult to guard. It was rare for any woman to
leave her teenage years and still be a virgin. A virgin has
always been one who is untainted and unaffected by the
vagaries of the secular world. The mind, imagination, and
spirit that are nurtured in an adult virgin body are seen as
something qualitatively different—and purer—than all others.

Protestants have questioned Mary's continued virginity
for centuries. It is uncommon to doubt that she was a virgin
at the time of the Annunciation, but she is often described
as having given birth to children after Jesus, or as having
had normal, sexual relations with Joseph throughout their
marriage. Catholic tradition says otherwise—and in the
strictest of terms.

The writers of the New Testament do not help in settling the issues, as they often seem to disagree on the most fundamental issues of faith. For example, who were Jesus' parents? Matthew's and Luke's Gospels offer genealogical clues for Jesus in the line of King David through Joseph, the husband of Mary. But Joseph's flesh had nothing to do with the boy's. In contrast to Matthew and Luke, Mark's Gospel offers no genealogy for Jesus at all, referring to him only as "the son of Mary," implying that there was no real father. John's Gospel does what it often does—takes the situation to a further, mystical, end. John has Jesus saying that God the Father is his only parent: "I came from the Father and have come into the world; again, I am leaving the world and am going to the Father." Finally, the author of the New Testament letter to the Hebrews teaches that Jesus was "Without father, without mother, without genealogy, having neither beginning of days nor end of life."[6]

What was the relationship between Mary's body and the Christ child? The Annunciation was the bringing of the news to Mary (and to humankind), but the second person of the Trinity existed before time began. Some of the more radical Protestant reformers taught that the Incarnation pre-existed the coming of Christ. This sort of doctrine would pull Christ out of human time, saying that the second person of the Trinity existed as a man from the foundation of the world, before the Creation itself, eternally one with the Father and the Holy Spirit. Medieval icons show the three persons of the Trinity all together, like a family; the Father is seated at the center, and beside him are the Son, often standing beside the Father, and the Holy Spirit, represented in a dove, hovering at the other side of the Father, facing forward. For those reformers, what would a Christ outside of history say about Mary, his mother? Did Mary, too, exist before time began? Was Christ somehow already enfleshed even before he had flesh, or was given flesh, by making his home in the strange heaven of Mary's womb?

So, when God came to grow as a human being inside of Mary's womb, whose flesh was it? The divine-human life that was Jesus Christ began with the aid of divine sperm or some other miraculous means of fertilizing Mary's egg, but it was Mary's flesh alone that grew the fetus. Christian mystics sometimes make this seem like a non-issue, as in this fantasy from one of Bernard of Clairvaux's sermons on the Song of Songs. Applying an allegorical interpretation to the words of the bride in the Song, he writes of Christ, "Look he comes, leaping upon the mountains, bounding over the hills." Bernard explains that this is Christ himself, leaping through space and time:

> For he bounded over Gabriel and preceded him to the Virgin, as the archangel himself witnesses when he says: 'Hail, Mary, full of grace . . .' What is this? He whom you just left in heaven do you now find in the womb? He flew, even flew ahead, on the wings of the wind.[7]

But while some medieval mystics were fuzzy on clarifying biological issues, other, more recent ones have interpreted Mary's role as absolutely central: "How I love you, Mary, you who made / This Divine Flower blossom on our shores!" (St. Thérèse of Lisieux).[8]

MEANINGS OF MOTHERHOOD

There have been plenty of metaphors for Mary's womb over the centuries. That "strange heaven" has also been compared to a tabernacle, an unopened gate, a sealed fountain, a tower, a holy field, a palace, blessed cloister, and a reliquary. God had an unusual home for those nine months, feeding on blood and partaking of flesh, while still very much of heaven. As we will see, Mary's blood and flesh, and even her breast-milk, became important clues to how Christians would perceive her role in the history of salvation, and her virginity inspired many to reinterpret the meaning of sex, procreation, and the ways of loving God.

Although Mary was not a surrogate mother, her role did include some surrogacy. In Western religious history, Sarah and Abraham were the first surrogate parents. Sarah found a birth mother in the person of Hagar, her Egyptian servant girl, in order to satisfy her and Abraham's desire to have a child. Sarah sent Abraham to sleep with Hagar, and the result was, frankly, disastrous. When Sarah could first tell that Hagar was pregnant, the Book of Genesis says that Sarah "looked with contempt on her." Hagar brought Ishmael to term for the old couple, but the boy was never really integrated into the family. Abraham had him circumcised when he was thirteen years old, a sign that he regarded him as a legitimate son, but a surrogate child was not good enough for Sarah and Abraham. Before long, Sarah was made miraculously pregnant with her firstborn, Isaac, and after he was born and weaned, she urged Abraham to send both Hagar and Ishmael away. Again, Genesis records that "Sarah saw the son of Hagar the Egyptian, whom she had borne to Abraham, playing with her son Isaac. So she said to Abraham, 'Cast out this slave woman with her son; for the son of this slave woman shall not inherit along with my son Isaac'" (21:9-10).

Any gestational surrogacy consultant today could have suggested various ways for Sarah and Abraham to avoid these pitfalls. But, the ancient couple's experience does point to some of the ethical issues related to the separation of sexual relations, procreation, and parenthood. Long ago,

Why a Virgin?

people first wrestled with what it means to be a mother or a father, and what makes a family.

The Virgin Mary was not a surrogate mother. It was her egg that produced the child, making her the genetic mother. And she was also the gestational mother, as it was Mary and only Mary who bore and gave birth to the child. But, just as it was not Sarah's egg that produced Ishmael, it was not Joseph's sperm that fertilized the zygote that became Jesus. Critics have often looked on Mary's role in the birth of Jesus as little more than a borrowed womb. One radical, Protestant reformer even argued that it was "impossible for the flesh of Christ to be formed of the seed of Mary." Orbe Philips was anxious to avoid all elements of Catholic religion in his rejection and reframing of Christian teaching. In the process, he became a heretic, saying, "God, the Heavenly Father, prepared for Jesus Christ . . . a body, but not of corrupt human seed, rather of his incorruptible seed."[9] According to both Catholic and Protestant theology, as well as surrogate ethics, Mary was a complete mother.

She said yes to God, and unlike many women of her age, she was not at the mercy of a man, usually the woman's father or husband, who would decide when she would become pregnant. It would be more accurate, in fact, to compare Mary to women today who seek practical means of exercising a wide range of fertility options such as egg banking, egg freezing, and using sperm donors. That is, of course, if we assume that Mary had the choice to say no to God at the Annunciation—and I believe that she did. Mary should be the patron saint of mothers, especially expectant and single mothers, although she isn't.

A scholar at Graduate Theological Union in Berkeley, California, recently compared Mary to the title character of Tina Turner's hit song, "Proud Mary," in order to demonstrate how people might view the Virgin today. "Mary is, I believe, a sociocultural figure who symbolizes the embodiment of a vibrant, wise woman with maternal and earthly instincts. . . . She is a sensual, sexual being who is most intimate with God."[10] As you can imagine, this sort of interpretation is at odds with traditional Catholic dogma, which usually emphasizes Mary's virginity as a series of renouncements, rather than fulfillments. Nevertheless, reinterpretations of Mary's sexuality are beginning to make sense to many people of faith. They lead us to ask: "Why is it important to the dogma of the Church that Mary never experienced sex, or even felt pain in childbirth?"

ST. AUGUSTINE AND HIS THEORY OF CONCUPISCENCE

We have to go back to Augustine of Hippo in order to understand how Mary's virginity has been perceived in the West over the centuries. Long before his death in AD 430, Augustine's ideas dominated the Christian world, and in many respects, they still do.

When the mighty Roman Empire, which ruled most of what is now Europe, Scandinavia, the British Isles, and North Africa, was summarily defeated by the invading Goths in 410, many people concluded that Christianity itself was to blame. The popular theory ran like this: Ever since the Christian faith became the "official" religion of the Empire one hundred years earlier by Constantine, the Empire had become weaker and weaker. Christian rulers forbade the worship of the old Roman, civic gods, and made Christianity the rule of the land, instead. Those earlier gods had helped preserve the Empire for many centuries before Constantine and Christianity put everything in jeopardy.

It was for the purpose of answering these accusations that Augustine wrote his classic apology for Christianity,

Why a Virgin?

The City of God. Augustine attempted to explain how Christians live in the earthly "city," while being citizens also in the heavenly "city." He wrote at length about issues such as the relationship between church and state, the obligations of a Christian to both religious and civil authority, the history of the civilized world and how Christianity had informed that history up until the mid-fifth century—and just about everything else in between! Augustine is still considered the supreme "Doctor" of the Western Church.

In the midst of all of this interpretive history, Augustine theorizes about what happened in the Garden of Eden when Adam and Eve committed the first sin. In Book 14, he says that when Adam and Eve first partook of the fruit of the forbidden tree, it was then, and only then, that they were ashamed of their nakedness. Before that first sin, Augustine explains, there may have been sex, but definitely no sexual enjoyment, in Eden. He explains that the sin of lust is equivalent to the pleasure of sex, even between husband and wife. Building on earlier writings of St. Jerome (who taught that marriage was intended only for those who had not the strength for virginity), Augustine coined a term for this lust: *concupiscence.*

Augustine argued that any sensible Christian, and any godly Christian, should want to procreate, when necessary, but without lust; for when a person allows him or herself sexual enjoyment, called "lust" by Augustine, "it moves the whole person, without and within, with such a mixture of mental emotion and carnal appetite that it becomes the highest bodily pleasure that can be produced."[11] Augustine is, of course, talking about orgasm. And, if you've ever read his other, more intriguing book, *The Confessions,* you know that Augustine has plenty of firsthand experience upon which to draw.

19

This marked the beginning, and became the linchpin, of Christian sexual ethics. As the most holy of humans, Mary was seen as the exemplar of a mother who created a son without tainting her flesh with sex. She also remained a virgin after Christ's birth. As Jerome wrote: "Christ and Mary, both virgins, consecrated the pattern of virginity for both sexes."[12] Hildegard of Bingen (d. 1179), the abbess and medieval mystic, later agreed with Augustine's doctrine and argued that Mary's womb remained always a "closed garden." She is the one who restored creation to the state it was in before the Fall: "Alleluia, O branch mediatrix . . . your womb illuminated all creatures with the beautiful flower born from the sweetest integrity, the modesty of your closed garden." Again using language that echoes the creation narrative in the Torah, Hildegard explains that whereas the first Eve "threw into chaos" the first Creation, Mary becomes through the sexless procreation of Christ, "a fountain springing from the Father's heart."[13]

John Milton, the great Protestant English poet of *Paradise Lost*, also took up this doctrine from Augustine and, as is the case with many of our ideas about the first parents and the events in the Garden of Eden, Milton's descriptions soon became better known than the biblical narrative itself. Milton describes in Book IX what was happening immediately after Adam and Eve ate the forbidden fruit:

> As with new wine intoxicated both,
> They swim in mirth, and fancy that they feel
> Divinity within them breeding wings,
> Wherewith to scorn the earth: But that false fruit
> Far other operation first displayed,
> Carnal desire inflaming; he on Eve
> Began to cast lascivious eyes; she him
> As wantonly repaid; in lust they burn . . .

Why a Virgin?

Augustine is also largely responsible for what is called the doctrine of original sin. By this, he meant that Adam and Eve transmitted their sinfulness to their children, and to their children's children, and so on forever. And so, literally—again, it boils down to sex for Augustine!—on each occasion when a man and a woman have intercourse and successfully create an offspring, the taint of sin and death is transmitted into that new, human life.

And so, you can see why it became so important to church theologians—following in Augustine's footsteps—that Mary not only never gave birth to a child other than Jesus, but also that she must not have experienced a normal childbirth when Jesus was born. Literally, the idea is that Mary's womb was never opened. She broke the cycle of concupiscence. As Augustine's contemporary, St. Proclus of Constantinople, said in a sermon in 446: "God formed Mary without a stain of her own, and so did the Christ proceed from her contracting no stain."

Another saint, Peter Chrysologus, preached the following explanation of these doctrines at about the time of Augustine's death:

> Other women's conceptions and giving birth occurs in bodies subject to passion; the Virgin Mary's conception and giving birth occurred in the tranquility of the divine Spirit and peace of the human body. Her blood was still, and the flesh astonished. Her private parts were entirely at rest, and her entire womb was quiescent during the visit of the Holy One. . . . The Virgin conceives, the Virgin brings forth her child, and she remains a virgin.

After Augustine, marriage without sex, without consummation, was presumed to be the purest form of love imaginable. Marriage without sex was thought to be unadulterated love. And then, for those living outside of marriage, virginity also became the ideal. The womb of Mary was sacred not only because God grew there, but also because it was planted with the seed of God, not man. A miracle of conception happened in that strange heaven of Mary. This consummation with God became a common expression among celibate women mystics during the Middle Ages. Many women—and occasionally some men— used erotic phrases from the Song of Songs to depict the sort of relationship that God has with and in them. These erotic terms replace the human with the divine.

For example, in one of her poems, Thérèse of Lisieux writes that Christ is her "Supreme Beauty" and she pines, "For you I must die." In another poem, Thérèse—who always emphasized the drama of her own life—explains that "the kiss of his mouth" is what actually, continually, gives her the treasures of chastity and virginity. Similarly, Mechthild of Magdeburg writes longingly in the first part of *The Flowing Light of the Godhead,* a recording of her visions: "Ah Lord! love me greatly, love me often and long! For the more continuously Thou lovest me, the purer I shall be. The more fervently Thou lovest me, the more lovely I shall be. The longer Thou lovest me the more holy I shall become, even here on earth." Throughout the history of Christianity, there has been a persistent quality that defines virgins, over and against the rest of humanity. There is a purity of mind, imagination, and spirit that deepens and broadens into God in those who have never been sexually active.

These celibate mystics use the language of sexual con-summation to describe their union with God in conscious imitation of Mary. They assume, with Jerome and Augustine and other early theologians, that sex taints the body. In fact, they also assumed that the body itself was somehow tainted from its very beginning, from the moment it emerged from the womb. That is why it was so important that Mary's womb would be unbroken and unopened as a result of the birth of Jesus, and that is also why it was impossible that Mary would have had sex with her husband throughout her life.

THE SAFETY OF MARY AS "VIRGIN"

Men—who represent ninety-nine percent of the authors who have praised Mary in print over the last two millennia— seem to love to focus on the beauty, charm, and grace of the little woman from Nazareth. (The writings of women rarely survived—a great loss to those of us, today, wanting to understand how Mary was perceived in the early centuries.) Pre-marital virginity, which is the only quality we seem to really know for certain about Mary from the initial description of her in the Gospels, takes on much greater proportions in the minds of the men who have admired her. The patristic and medieval commentators on Scripture clearly wanted Mary to be the ideal woman, right down to physical type.

Epiphanius, a Western monk who lived and wrote during the Roman Empire, explained with great certainty in one of his treatises: "Her complexion was the color of ripe wheat, and her hair was auburn. Her eyes were bright and keen, and light brown in color, and the pupils were of an olive-green tint. Her eyebrows were arched and deep black. Her nose was long, her lips were red and full, and overflowing with the sweetness of words. Her face was not round, but somewhat oval. Her hands were long and her fingers also."[14] Epiphanius would not be the first, or the last, monk to spend too much time meditating on the physical beauty of the mother of God. Albertus Magnus (ca. 1200–80), the teacher of Thomas Aquinas in Paris, wrote many pages about Mary's physical beauty, as if that mattered and as if it was knowable. When he wrote his commentary on the Song of Songs, he saw Mary in the figure of the beautiful woman depicted there. Song of Songs 1:15, for instance, reads, "Ah, you are beautiful, my love; ah, you are beautiful; your eyes are doves." Albertus Magnus went on to explain that every part of Mary's body—including her shoulders, lips, and feet—were lovely.

Albertus Magnus was not alone in interpreting the Song of Songs as a love poem of marriage between the Holy Spirit and Mary. It was common during the Middle Ages for men to see, through the lens of this mystical text, how God the Father would desire this fair virgin and would make God's Son with her. In his classic reference, *History of the Christian Church*, Protestant scholar Philip Schaff notes that another monk, Eberhard of Saxony, wrote exactly this as praise of Mary's beauty: "God on His throne desired thy beauty and wanted / O crown of womanhood / to look on thee with passion." Bonaventure, one of the earliest biographers of St. Francis of Assisi, wrote: "Hail to you, heavenly lily. Hail to you, most graceful rose." In his *Paradiso*, canto xxxi, Dante wrote of Mary's lovely smile and charms beyond expression. We find none of this in the Bible.

Men have always been entranced by the possibility of the perpetual virginity of Mary, as well. Ambrose of Milan, the great teacher of Augustine, interprets one of the prophecies of Ezekiel as telling of Mary, God, and her virginity forever. Ezekiel 44:2–4 reads: "And he said to me, 'This gate shall remain shut; it shall not be opened, and no one shall enter by it; for the LORD, the God of Israel, has entered by it; therefore it shall remain shut. Only the prince may sit in it to eat bread before the LORD; he shall enter by way of the vestibule of the gate, and shall go out by the same way.'

Why a Virgin?

Then he brought me by way of the north gate to the front of the temple; and I looked, and behold, the glory of the LORD filled the temple of the LORD; and I fell upon my face" (RSV). To Ambrose, Mary's womb and chastity are that gate.

Mary's perpetual virginity was defended at various church councils, such as the Fifth Ecumenical Council held in Constantinople in 553. There, Mary was declared "ever-virgin" and it became an official anathema to deny it. (Some earlier church fathers, such as Tertullian, had denied it. Martin Luther, however, the greatest Protestant Reformer, upheld it.) The Sixth Ecumenical Council in 681, also held at Constantinople, accepted this as dogma that did not require further discussion.

What does it literally mean that Mary did not experience childbirth in the normal ways? According to the traditional metaphors, as we have seen, Mary remains an unopened gate, a sealed fountain, a reliquary with sacred contents, but closed to the outside. To put it into anatomical terms, it is important to Catholic teaching that Mary's hymen was unbroken by Christ's birth. Her virginity had to remain completely intact. As early as the second century, this teaching was present in the apocryphal gospel of Mary known as *The Book of James*. And according to the nativity tale in that unusual document, Joseph went out in search of a midwife who might help in the birthing of Jesus. Anxious to appear righteous, for he was much older than the sixteen-year-old Mary and he was known to have been entrusted to care for her as a virgin, Joseph explained to the midwife that Mary had conceived by the Holy Spirit, and not by any man. And so the midwife came with Joseph to see Mary in the cave, but she did not believe his story. Within minutes, according to the pace of the narrative, the midwife experienced various small miracles. In that cave as Mary quietly gave birth, there was an overshadowing "luminous cloud," and a mysterious "great light" that was so bright that everyone had to close their eyes. As the light faded away, the baby effortlessly "appeared" and took his mother's breast. The midwife cried out: "This is a great mystery to me, because I have seen this strange sight!" And she went out to tell someone.

Salome—presumably a friend of the midwife's who was also a midwife—was reluctant to believe the first woman's story. Salome is the "doubting Thomas" in this apocryphal nativity tale. She said to her friend: "As the Lord my God liveth, unless I thrust in my finger, and search the parts, I will not believe that a virgin has brought forth." The text continues: "And the midwife went in, and said to Mary: 'Show thyself; for no small controversy has arisen about thee.' And Salome put in her finger, and cried out, and said: 'Woe is me for mine iniquity and mine unbelief, because I have tempted the living God; and, behold, my hand is dropping off as if burned with fire.'" The story of these two midwives was an attempt by the ancient author to set the question to rest forever: Mary's perpetual virginity was literally intact.

In the fourteenth century, St. Bridget of Sweden even argued, in recounted visions that were read or discussed by perhaps millions of her contemporaries, that Christ was born effortlessly. Later, *The Gospel of the Birth of Mary* (see chapter 4) explains about the birth of Jesus: "But there has been no spilling of blood in his birth, no pain in bringing him forth. A virgin has conceived, a virgin has brought forth, and a virgin she remains."[15]

The Virgin Birth is not where the miracles of Mary's body ended. There are also many mystical meanings of virginity that Mary partook of. Her breasts flowed with milk, for instance, and she gave Christ a virgin's milk—better food than had ever been given to a child before. According to tradition, Mary's breasts flowed with the richest and purest of milk that the world has ever seen.

Why a Virgin?

As the birth-mother of the Church, the New Jerusalem, Mary was believed to be the fulfillment of this prophecy from Isaiah: "For thus says the LORD: I will extend prosperity to her like a river, and the wealth of the nations like an overflowing stream; and you shall nurse and be carried on her arm, and dandled on her knees" (Isaiah 66:12). One of her popular titles is even Our Lady of Perpetual Succor, as she was always ready to feed the baby, Jesus, and by extension, to care for all Christians as a good mother would. Catholic prayers and novenas to Mary as Our Lady of Perpetual Succor mirror very closely how Protestants often pray exclusively to Christ, at the moment or beginning of salvation. These prayers to Mary begin with the unworthiness of the sinner to be her child (just as prayer to Christ often begins with an admission of sin); then the devotee will ask for Mary's grace, despite unworthiness, to protect, defend, and nurture him or her as one of her children; and, finally, the prayer will conclude in a certain confidence that Mary's grace will be sufficient to support human frailty and instill faithfulness to Christ, and the devoted one will return to Mary thanks and praise forever.

It was common during the Middle Ages to see images of Mary lactating for the Christ child, her breast exposed, and nipple erect. This symbolized her gifts to Christ, but it also symbolized Mary as a divine mother who was prepared to succor anyone in need. Women mystics of the Middle Ages took the lactating role of Mary to greater depths in their own experiences. St. Christine the Astonishing, for instance, was a combination of holy fool, schizophrenic, and saint in what is now Belgium. Her oral teachings were pulled together by Thomas of Cantimpre, who related her bizarre stories of death, resurrection, living in treetops, and other strange behavior. According to Christine's and Thomas's account, there was a time in Christine's life when she loathed the presence of other people. She lived alone in the wilderness, in trees, churches, and on the tops of mountains. Her family, trying to free her from what appeared to be madness, bound her in iron chains, effectively straitjacketing her, but soon she escaped and fled in order to be alone. This time, she eventually became hungry and considered willingly returning home, if for no other reason than for food. But then, she experienced a miracle of the Virgin Mary, which in her chronicle, is taken to be a sure sign of sainthood in virginity:

> So she humbly prayed that [the Lord] would look mercifully upon her. . . . And then, straight away, she looked down at the dry breasts of her virgin bosom and saw them dropping sweet milk, quite contrary to what happens naturally. This is an astonishing thing, unheard of since the incomparable and unparalleled virgin, Christ's mother. And so the virgin Christine was fed for nine weeks with milk from her own breasts.[16]

Mechthild of Magdeburg writes in a vision that Mary's milk "nurtured the wise men and prophets before the birth of the Son of God." Then, according to the words of Mary, as given to Mechthild, "After that, in my youth, I nurtured Jesus; later, as the bride of God, I nurtured holy Church at the foot of the Cross; but from that I became dry and wretched, for the sword of the human agony of Jesus spiritually pierced my soul."[17]

THE REAL MEANING OF VIRGINITY?

Seventy-five years ago, in the heyday of psychoanalysis, spiritual experience was routinely diagnosed as psychosis, and the voluntary selection of a life of virginity was commonly

28

understood as a form of self-hatred. Today, there are deeper understandings of why one might choose to remain chaste, and they have little to do with self-denial and more to do with real self-understanding. By examining these, we may see Mary in a new light.

A woman who has consecrated her life to God alone, becomes a virgin without reduction. She is married to God, and the understanding of that relationship is often similar to the relationship between a husband and a wife. According to the testimony of many virgins through the ages, God becomes more than a source of faith, but also the source of desire and passion that animates all creative activity, replacing the human need for sex. Hildegard of Bingen (d. 1179), the Benedictine abbess and visionary, explained virginity by means of various of these metaphors in her *Antiphons to the Virgin*:

> O sweetest Lover!
> O sweetest Enfolder!
> help us to guard
> our virginity.
> We are joined to You in a marriage of your blood,
> rejecting men
> and choosing You, Son of God.
> O most beautiful Form!
> O most sweet savor of desirable delight!
> We ever sigh after You. . . .

In another song, Hildegard reflects again on the meaning of virginity:

> O how great is the happiness
> in this form
> because malice,

having flowed from Woman,
a woman later washed away
and gathered all the sweetly smelling virtues
and adorned Heaven
more than she had disordered Earth.[18]

The notion of sex being inherently bad, as it is of this earth and not of heaven, is still present in Hildegard's *Antiphons*, but nevertheless, we see more clearly through them to a virginity that is life-giving, joyful, and aimed at intellectual growth and good work in the world. Protestant scholars of the Bible are often interested in debunking the Catholic theory that Mary never had sex, and that she never experienced normal childbirth. But, there are other, more important ways, to expand on these Marian traditions.

Feminist religion scholar Mary Daly has centered her academic career around the re-defining of words that we thought we already knew. She defines *virgin* this way: "Wild, Lusty, Never captured, Unsubdued Old Maid; Marriage Resister."[19] Although intentionally provocative—aiming at the prejudices of men—Daly might be closer to the truth than we sometimes think. If Mary's virginity was life-giving and fruitful, wild and unsubdued, her spirit becomes all the more appealing for us today, and her wisdom all the more penetrating, as well.

2

A Legend Foretold by the Hebrew Prophets

Therefore the Lord himself
will give you a sign.
Look, the young woman is with child
and shall bear a son,
and shall name him Immanuel.
—Isaiah 7:14

*T*HIS IS THE BEST KNOWN OF THE OLD TESTAMENT
prophecies believed by Christians to be fulfilled in
the Annunciation to Mary. But it was by no means
the only literary connection between the very special Son of
Israel and God's redeeming plan in the New Testament.

The first Jewish Christians who heard the story of Jesus
as the Messiah were prepared to hear it as a result of generations of allusions in the Hebrew Scriptures and teaching in
the synagogues. The Annunciation is full of allusions to earlier
stories. For example, Isaac was born to Abraham and Sarah
after an angel came to tell Abraham to his great surprise:

"Your wife Sarah shall have a son." Samuel, too, was born to Hannah under miraculous circumstances such as these. Both stories were in the mind and imagination of the first Jewish Christians when they heard about the archangel Gabriel's coming to Mary in Luke's Gospel, saying to her: "Greetings, favored one! The Lord is with you." Centuries earlier, in Jewish tradition, the prophet Zephaniah had exclaimed: "Sing aloud, O daughter Zion; shout, O Israel! . . . The LORD, your God, is in your midst" (Zephaniah 3:14, 17). The nation of Israel, "the daughter of Zion," was waiting the arrival of the Messiah, and the Gospel of Luke used these images to convey the uniqueness of the birth of Jesus.

The Hebrew Bible is full of possible archetypes and prefigurings of Mary. Matthew and Luke, in particular, imaginatively linked these ancient prophecies to the events of the Nativity, as a way of proclaiming the special identity and purpose of Jesus the Christ. However, one must wear Christian lenses in order to see the Jewish Scriptures this way. Monsignor Ronald Knox, a popular Catholic theologian from the first half of the twentieth century, states the case most boldly:

> The Old Testament is, largely, a record of barbarian times. . . . But through this tangled skein runs a single golden thread; between these soiled pages lies, now and again, a pressed flower that has lost neither its color nor its sweetness. That thread, that flower, is the mention, by type and analogue, of her whom all generations of Christendom have called blessed, the Virgin of Virgins, the Queen of Heaven, the holy Mother of God.[20]

A Legend Foretold by the Hebrew Prophets

The most ancient reference among the Hebrew images for Mary is the title "New Eve." As the first woman, as well as the one who committed the first sin against God, Eve is viewed as the mother of mortality while Mary is seen as the mother of new life. (It should be noted that many scholars see Eve as an allegorical symbol, while Mary was a real person.) The Latin Church Fathers were the first ones to make this narrative connection popular at the time of the Roman Empire.

Augustine of Hippo: "Eve by her disobedience merited punishment, Mary by obeying obtained glory." "The first man, by persuasion of a virgin, fell, the Second Man, with consent of a Virgin, triumphed." "An evil angel of old seduced Eve, a good angel likewise encouraged Mary." "Eve perished by a word; to the Word likewise did Mary commit herself." Ambrose of Milan: "By the woman folly, by the Virgin wisdom." Jerome: "Death by Eve; life by Mary."

A popular Latin hymn from the same era translates this way: "Take up that *Ave* [*Ave* meaning "Hail," short for the "Hail Mary" prayer] from the mouth of Gabriel, and, reversing the name of Eva, establish us in peace."[21] The medieval imagination saw it as no accident that *Ave* was *Eva* (Latin for Eve), spelled backwards; in the same way, they believed, Mary reversed things, bringing redemption to all people, including the original sinner, Eve. The ancient belief in Mary's sinlessness also linked her to Eve, and to the promise of a restoration of what was in the Garden of Eden. She was a reminder to ancient and medieval Christians that an untarnished goodness is possible in humankind. Then, in a sweeping picture of history from the Garden to the Cross, it was believed that as the first Eve was seduced by a serpent, the second Eve would bring about the One who would finally crush the serpent's head.

JEROME'S MISTAKE— THE PROTO-EVANGELION

For many spiritual commentators during the early Middle Ages, the first foreshadowing of the Virgin Mary happened right in the Garden of Eden—or, at least, on the outskirts of it, immediately after the Fall when God forced Adam and Eve to leave Eden for the harsher world outside. According to a tradition initiated by St. Jerome in the fourth century, this is called the Proto-Evangelion, which means, "before the Good News."

In Genesis chapter three, God proclaims to the serpent— who deceived the first woman and man—"I will put enmities between you and the woman, and between your offspring and hers; he will strike your head, and you will strike his heel." That phrasing is from the modern New Revised Standard Version. But the most common translation for this verse during the Middle Ages came from Jerome's Latin Vulgate. It is as follows:

> I will put enmities between thee and the woman,
> And thy seed and her seed;
> She shall crush thy head, and thou shalt lie in wait for
> her heel.

The change in meaning from Jerome's Vulgate to today's modern translations is unmistakable. According to Jerome's Proto-Evangelion, Mary becomes even more fully—and wrongly—the "new Eve," the one who would one day even crush the head of Satan. Jerome made mistakes in his other-wise groundbreaking translation (the first to translate the

Scriptures into Latin, which was the language of the people in the fourth century), and theologians began pointing these out less than a generation after his death. In this case, because Jerome's Vulgate became the official version of the Bible used by the Church for many centuries, the mistake led to at least a millennium of doctrinal confusion.

In the New Revised Standard Version's rendering, which is representative of all modern translations today, God says to the serpent, "he will strike your head," referring to Christ, the son of Mary, rather than to Mary herself. But, Jerome translated this passage as if Mary herself would do the striking down of the serpent, or Satan. For centuries, Jerome's mistake led to confusion about Mary and her powers. For instance, if Mary could perform such salvific heroics as striking down the head of Satan, she must also be without sin. The doctrine of the Immaculate Conception would probably never have arisen if it were not for Jerome's mistake (more on this later, in chapter 11). As a result, we see the first attribution of spiritual power to Mary—power that belonged to her Son alone.

"BLESSED ARE YOU"

She was pronounced "blessed" by her cousin, Elizabeth (and at the Annunciation by the archangel Gabriel, according to an addition put in by the translators of the King James Version), and there is perhaps no word that has come to define her more than this one. She is consecrated, made holy, one of the fortunate under God's care.

"Blessed" links Mary to her Jewish forebears. Moses said to the people Israel: "If you will only obey the LORD your God. . . . Blessed shall be the fruit of your womb, the fruit of your ground, and the fruit of your livestock," in Deuteronomy 28:1 and 4. "Most blessed of women be Jael, the wife of Heber the Kenite, of tent-dwelling women most blessed," says Judges 5:24. And Uzziah praised Judith for cutting off the head of Nebuchadnezzar's top general, saying, "O daughter, you are blessed by the Most High God above all other women on earth" (Judith 13:18). In Hebrew, to bless is to praise, and so the Hebrews would praise God by blessing God, which also implied giving him thanks.

"Blessed are you among women," Elizabeth says, and then Mary herself resounds, "Surely, from now on all generations will call me blessed" (Luke 1:42, 48). Mary is one of these great women of Israel, of the covenantal people, in the line of the kings of Israel, from which will come the promised Messiah. But she is clearly more than that, too. She is a culmination of the adjective of God's action, "blessed." She is also blesséd—the continuous past tense of that action, but more than that: a worthy object of human veneration.

Jacobus de Voragine's popular hagiographic text, *The Golden Legend*, even has Mary singing on her deathbed about herself, repeating her Magnificat aloud for all to hear. After that, according to Jacobus, a cantor intoned a response in a higher pitch, and then Mary returned: "Behold I come! In the head of the book it is written of me that I should do thy will, O God, because my spirit has rejoiced in thee, God my Savior."[22] Immediately, then, Mary died.

Daughter of Zion and Poor of the Lord

Both of these names link Mary to the house of Israel and express her role in connecting the old covenant with the new. She is never called Daughter of Zion in the pages of the New Testament, but the parallels between passages in the Hebrew prophets such as Zephaniah correspond very closely to the language in the Gospel of Luke. In the Annunciation,

A Legend Foretold by the Hebrew Prophets

Luke deliberately linked Mary with the Daughter of Zion, described by the prophets of Israel:

Sing aloud, O daughter of Zion; shout, O Israel!	"Greetings, favored one! The Lord is with you. . . .
Rejoice and exult with all your heart. . . .	"Do not be afraid, Mary, for you have found favor with
The king of Israel, the Lord, is in your midst; you shall fear disaster no more. . . .	God. And now, you will conceive in your womb and bear a son, and you will name
The Lord, your God, is in your midst. . . . [H]e will renew you in his love.	him Jesus. He will be great, and will be called the Son of the Most High."
—Zephaniah 3:14–17	—Luke 1:28–31

The Daughter of Zion meant Jerusalem, and then, later, the people of Israel themselves. She was like a virgin waiting, full of hope for the birth of a child. She was like Mary.

Mary's connection to the poor of the Lord is based on her own humble circumstances. The birth of Jesus and the flight into Egypt are two examples of how Mary lived far from wealth and privilege. In fact, in the flight, the Holy Family resembles today's refugees, wandering without home and in search of a place of safety.

The phrase, "the poor of the Lord" is mentioned by the prophets Zephaniah (3:12) and Isaiah (66:2) and refers to a spiritual remnant in Israel, the humbled who will one day be exalted. Jesus was probably remembering these poor of the Lord when he preached the Beatitudes in his Sermon on the Mount. Jesus went into the synagogue on the Sabbath in Nazareth and read these words from the prophet Isaiah: "The Spirit of the Lord is upon me, because he has anointed me to bring good news to the poor" (Luke 4:18). Many commentators have attached and extended this title to

Mary, as well, and she is still believed by millions to be the greatest spiritual champion of the poor.

The Ark of the Covenant

Mary is also imagined in the New Testament as one who is protected by God—and who, in turn, protects God. Just as the cherubim and the cloud were made to protect the ark of the (first) covenant, Mary was the ark of Jesus, the new covenant. She was able to do this only by divine assistance. God said to Moses on Mount Sinai: "You shall make two cherubim of gold. . . . The cherubim shall spread out their wings above, overshadowing the mercy seat with their wings" (Exodus 25:18, 20). And "the cloud of the Lord was on the tabernacle by day, and fire was in the cloud by night, before the eyes of all the house of Israel" (Exodus 40:38). So, too, does the Holy Spirit "overshadow" Mary. "The angel said to her, 'The Holy Spirit will come upon you, and the power of the Most High will overshadow you; therefore the child to be born will be holy; he will be called Son of God'" (Luke 1:35).

Likewise, Mary is the new ark for grace. Noah's ark saved humanity from calamity, while Mary's ark, her womb, provided sanctuary for the new covenant of God that came through Jesus. This may have reminded the first readers of the Gospels of the conclusion of the Book of Exodus, when *Shekinah*, a feminine mystery of God's presence, is pictured as covering the ark of the covenant. "Then the cloud covered the tent of meeting, and the glory of the LORD filled the tabernacle. Moses was not able to enter the tent of meeting because the cloud settled upon it, and the glory of the LORD filled the tabernacle. Whenever the cloud was taken up from the tabernacle, the Israelites would set out on each stage of their journey; but if the cloud was not taken up, then they did not set out until the day that it was taken up. For the cloud of the LORD was on the tabernacle by day, and fire was in the cloud by night, before the eyes of all the house of Israel at each stage of their journey" (Exodus 40:34–38). Such images signal Mary's power.

MORE METAPHORS

Mary has many other historically significant qualities according to Christian interpretations of the Old Testament. Sarah was the mother of Isaac, who then fathered Jacob, and who then became "Israel." Mary later became *mother of the new Israel*. But Mary's faith was an improvement over Sarah's, who according to the text, laughed at the notion of her giving birth at such an advanced age. Mary, on the other hand, rejoiced and had immediate faith in the words of the archangel.

Mary also became the *new ladder of Jacob*. Jacob's famous dream of angels going up and down to heaven on a wondrous ladder later became an image of the intercession of Mary for sinners. Through her, our prayers not only go up to the heavens, but they return to us with answers and assurances. We no longer have to wrestle with the angels, as Jacob once did; we may intercede to Christ through his mother, Mary.

Hannah also prefigures Mary. Hannah offered her first son, Samuel, to God to work in the temple, while Mary gave her only son, Jesus, as the new temple. Hannah pleaded so often in the temple for a son that the chief priest, Eli, finally assumed that she must be a vagrant drunk. Mary, who was from a poor family that had come down in the world by many degrees, did not ask but was given a son by God's grace.

The prophet Jeremiah prefigures the role of the Virgin Mary as one who is caring for us, who cries tears for us, and is ready to help us before the Divine. The prophet's words again foreshadow Luke's words depicting the women who followed Jesus during his time of passion. "Thus says the Lord of hosts: Consider, and call for the mourning women to come; send for the skilled women to come; let them quickly raise a dirge over us, so that our eyes may run down with tears, and our eyelids flow with water" (Jeremiah 9:17-18). We need the tears and the help of a mother.

ECHOES OF MARY
IN THE BOOK OF PSALMS

The canticles of Mary, such as the Magnificat, are echoed in some of the Hebrew psalms of thanksgiving and praise. Chief among these are two psalms, in particular. Psalm 8 reminds us of Mary's praise for God at the announcement of the Annunciation.

1. O LORD our Governor,
how exalted is your Name in all the world!
2. Out of the mouths of infants and children
your majesty is praised above the heavens.
3. You have set up a stronghold against your adversaries, to quell the enemy and the avenger.
4. When I consider your heavens, the work of your fingers, the moon and the stars you have set in their courses,
5. What is man that you should be mindful of him? the son of man that you should seek him out?
6. You have made him but little lower than the angels; you adorn him with glory and honor;
7. You give him mastery over the works of your hands; you put all things under his feet:
8. All sheep and oxen,

even the wild beasts of the field,

⁹· The birds of the air, the fish of the sea,
and whatsoever walks in the paths of the sea.

¹⁰· O LORD our Governor,
how exalted is your Name in all the world!
(Psalm 8 - BCP)

And Psalm 90 sings with the desires of every Christian who wants to model him or herself after the humility, patience, and wisdom of the Virgin.

¹·Lord, you have been our refuge
from one generation to another.

²·Before the mountains were brought forth,
or the land and the earth were born,
from age to age you are God.

³·You turn us back to the dust and say,
"Go back, O child of earth."

⁴·For a thousand years in your sight are like yesterday
when it is past and like a watch in the night.

⁵·You sweep us away like a dream;
we fade away suddenly like the grass.

⁶·In the morning it is green and flourishes;
in the evening it is dried up and withered.

⁷·For we consume away in your displeasure;
we are afraid because of your wrathful indignation.
⁸·Our iniquities you have set before you,
and our secret sins in the light of your countenance.

⁹·When you are angry, all our days are gone;
we bring our years to an end like a sigh.

[10.] The span of our life is seventy years,
perhaps in strength even eighty;
yet the sum of them is but labor and sorrow,
for they pass away quickly and we are gone.

[11.] Who regards the power of your wrath?
who rightly fears your indignation?

[12.] So teach us to number our days
that we may apply our hearts to wisdom.

[13.] Return, O LORD; how long will you tarry?
be gracious to your servants.

[14.] Satisfy us by your loving-kindness in the morning;
so shall we rejoice and be glad all the days of our
life.

[15.] Make us glad by the measure of the days that
you afflicted us and the years in which we suffered
adversity.

[16.] Show your servants your works
and your splendor to their children.

[17.] May the graciousness of the LORD our God be
upon us; prosper the work of our hands;
prosper our handiwork.
(Psalm 90 - BCP)

THE MYSTICAL BRIDE AND HER BRIDEGROOM

For mystics throughout the Middle Ages, Mary was
also seen in the figure of the bride of the Song of Songs.
Betrothed to God the Holy Spirit in order to create Jesus out
of that beautiful, heavenly union, Mary is the mystical bride
of the heavenly Bridegroom. Some mystics even took the
comparison further, wedding Mary to God the Father after

the Fall, as part of the divine plan not yet revealed. Others wrote of Mary wedded to God soon after the foundation of the world itself, or, to extend the metaphor to its fullest, wedding her to God the Trinity.

Listen to Mechthild of Magdeburg, the influential thirteenth-century German Dominican. She is recounting the words of Mary herself, as they were given to her in a vision:

> When our Father's joy was darkened by Adam's fall, so that He was an-angered, the everlasting wisdom of Almighty God was provoked. Then the Father chose me as bride that He might have something to love, because His noble bride, the soul, was dead. Then the Son chose me as mother and the Holy Spirit received me as friend.[23]

This is a further example of Mary's intrinsic worth in medieval tradition. She is not contained by a summary of her qualities, or activities. We cannot simply call her *ark of the new covenant, new ladder of Jacob*, and so on. She possesses essential value, a native identity similar only to that of gods, before her time, but extended then to human beings, after her.

CHAPTER 3

Was Mary the First Disciple? (the Gospels)

And the child's father and mother were amazed
at what was being said about him.
Then Simeon blessed them and said to his mother,
Mary, "This child is destined for the falling
and the rising of many in Israel, and to be a sign
that will be opposed so that the inner
thoughts of many will be revealed—
and a sword will pierce your own soul too."
—Luke 2:34-35

WHAT DID SHE FIRST SAY, AT THE Annunciation, when the archangel Gabriel arrived unannouced to tell her that she had been specially chosen by God? Mary does not sound like a ready-made disciple. She is not the cookie-cut, already perfect mold into which God was poured. In effect, Mary said: "What?!"

The text in Luke's Gospel (1:26–38) is full of words of hesitancy. "In the sixth month the angel Gabriel was sent by God to a town in Galilee called Nazareth, to a virgin engaged to a man whose name was Joseph, of the house of David. The virgin's name was Mary.

"And he came to her and said, 'Greetings, favored one! The Lord is with you.' "But she was much perplexed. . . . pondered . . . afraid . . . How can this be?"

Sometime after her shock subsided, she actually then said: "Here am I, the servant of the Lord; let it be with me according to your word." She believed, and in so believing, became the first true disciple of her as yet unborn son. Even so, she was the first person in the New Testament Gospel accounts to show us that belief does not come without some measure of question and doubt. Centuries of tradition have tended to erase that fact, making the images of Mary into unerring and unflinching gazes of certitude, but don't believe it. No. Mary is the chief disciple because she shows us how to wait on God, expect God, have awe for God, and hope for God, but not with an easy credulity. Hers was not an unquestioning belief; these qualities are, instead, the qualities of a mature disciple. And for Mary, these expectations of awe and hope began at about the age of thirteen!

Her verbal consent was in itself, innovative. In the Hebrew Bible when God comes calling, asking one of his people to do something, there is never a depiction of verbal consent. It is as if such a response is completely unnecessary. In contrast, Mary hears, questions, and responds as if to stand up and say "Yes, here I am."

St. Bernardino of Siena, a fifteenth-century preacher, once explained that it was Gabriel, and not Mary, who was dumbfounded by—or, just simply dumb—in the face of what was being said at the Annunciation. According to Bernardino, Gabriel didn't know much of anything about what he had been sent to tell the girl. By her questions and confident responses, Mary "confounds the beautiful, dumb blond creature who has just flown into her life with his extraordinary news. . . . [I]t is all too subtle for Gabriel's angelic brain to grasp."[24]

"MY SOUL MAGNIFIES THE LORD"

Mary's story does not begin with the Magnificat, but it is actually the theological beginning and ending of her story. In those few lines, Mary not only prefigures the message to be preached by her son, Jesus, but she prefigures the gospel message itself. The word *Magnificat* is Latin and means "magnifies," as in the first line of the famous prayer: "My soul magnifies the Lord." According to the sentence structure of Latin, the word *Magnificat* comes first: "*Magnificat anima mea Dominum.*" Mary's words are a simple theology, a summary of many of the themes from the Hebrew prophets and psalms, and then later preached by Jesus himself. God

* saves us.
* regards and exalts the lowly.
* is mighty and holy.
* shows mercy to those who understand his power.
* causes us to be separated from each other by pride.
* fills the hungry with good things.
* leaves the rich empty-handed.
* regards his people with mercy.

Luke is the kindest to Mary of all of the New Testament writers. She actually speaks (the Magnificat) in Luke's Gospel, unlike Matthew's, and Luke is also the only one to show the later scene of Mary and Joseph looking for Jesus in the temple.

But it is not just Mary's soul that magnifies the Lord, as a result of the Annunciation. The human soul does, too. According to tradition, the Annunciation was brought to Mary, and the Christ child was born, in order that the human soul might be reconciled to God. It is for this reason that the baby Jesus is sometimes pictured in paintings and sculptures as holding a dove while sitting on Mary's lap. Sometimes, he is even playing with the bird, which again represents the mystical love story of the Song of Songs, where the Bridegroom (God) says to the bride (us), "Open to me, my sister, my love, my dove, my perfect one" (5:2). That bird represents the soul of humankind; we all could sing the Magnificat!

Was Mary the First Disciple? (the Gospels)

To magnify means to enlarge or expand. How is it possible that a simple soul, such as Mary or any of the rest of humanity, might enlarge the God who does all that she speaks of? Quite simply, our words and actions do the magnifying.

The Greatest Disciple

Not only did Mary give birth to Jesus, and not only was she the first person to have faith in him and his mission, but also she was the one who presented Jesus to the world. As we see in icons all around the world—particularly in those called *Hodegetria*, or, "she who shows the way"—Mary is pictured as gesturing with her hand toward the Christ child on her lap, while her eyes remain focused ahead, looking at the viewer. But, such a scene is never described in Scripture. For this, we turn to one of only two scenes from the life of Mary in the fourth Gospel (the other depicts her standing at the foot of the cross), the wedding at Cana.

Although modern scholars express doubt, the Catholic Church and Christian tradition assign the authorship of the fourth Gospel, along with the Book of Revelation, to the "Beloved Disciple" who was known as John. Strangely, this last of the canonical Gospels to be written does not share any of the other stories of Mary that occur in the synoptic Gospels of Matthew, Mark, and Luke. None of them. It is as if John either did not know the earlier accounts, or, he was attempting to transmit a different part of the gospel tradition. Also unusual is the fact that Mary is not known by her name in John's Gospel; she is known simply as the mother of Jesus.

It seems to be less important to John that Jesus and his disciples were present at this first miracle, as opposed to Mary. He writes, "[T]here was a wedding in Cana of Galilee, and the mother of Jesus was there. Jesus and his disciples had also been invited to the wedding." The set-up to the story makes it clear that this is something about Mary, as much as it is about Jesus. The point being made is that Mary chose the time when Jesus would begin revealing himself to the world. She comes to him, as the wine runs out, and asks him to do something about it. Jesus replies, "Woman, what concern is that to you and to me? My hour has not yet come." And as Mary walks away, saying to the house servants, "Do whatever he tells you," it is as if she winks, nods, or touches the arm of her son to say, "It is time."

After the wedding at Cana, there is no place better than the scene of the "upper room," after Christ's ascension to heaven from Mount Olivet, to see the role that Mary played among the followers of Christ. The eleven remaining disciples did not know what to do. They were confused, afraid, and uncertain. Jesus had asked them to wait in Jerusalem and to wait on the Lord in prayer, according to Acts, chapter one: "While staying with them [during the forty days between the Resurrection and the Ascension], [Jesus] ordered them not to leave Jerusalem, but to wait there for the promise of the Father." We know that they were reading the Hebrew

The Virgin Mary and the Apostle John as witnesses to the violence of the Cross, from an eleventh-century mosaic.

Scriptures together in that upper room, as well as praying for God's will and direction. They also elected the twelfth apostle, a replacement for the traitor, Judas.

The disciples, Mary, and possibly Mary Magdalene, stayed together in that house in Jerusalem and discussed what had happened. Tradition has it that this waiting lasted for nine days as the group sought God's will and wisdom. During this time, Mary was probably considered to be the most important person in the room. Aside from knowing Jesus the best, Mary was also the most important of the women who stayed by Christ's side during the Passion and Crucifixion. All four of the Gospels agree that a group of women were there, following him and keeping vigil, as the texts also suggest that the male disciples quickly scattered in fear and confusion. In John's account, Mary stood beside the beloved disciple, presumably John himself, bearing witness to the horrendous events during Jesus' last hours. "Women standing near the cross or at a distance kept the death watch, their faithfulness a sign to Jesus that not all relationships had been broken, despite his feeling of intense abandonment even by God," explains Elizabeth A. Johnson.[25] And Mary was chief among these women. As mothers often do today in countries around the world, Mary insisted on bearing witness to the crimes and violence that took the life of her son. Nine days after the Ascension—following this period of waiting on God—came the outpouring of the Holy Spirit, celebrated in today's churches as the day of Pentecost.

Strange Heaven

The last word from the Gospels about Mary is this one, from chapter nineteen of John's Gospel:

> Meanwhile, standing near the cross of Jesus were his mother, and his mother's sister, Mary the wife of Clopas, and Mary Magdalene. When Jesus saw his mother and the disciple whom he loved standing beside her, he said to his mother, 'Woman, here is your son.' Then he said to the disciple, 'Here is your mother.' And from that hour the disciple took her into his own home." (John 19:26-27)

St. Thérèse of Lisieux heightens the importance of Mary's role at the foot of the cross, and not just as the most important disciple. In one of her poems, she wrote: "Mary, at the top of Calvary standing beside the Cross / To me you seem like a priest at the altar, / Offering your beloved Jesus, the sweet Emmanuel."[26]

What happened after Jesus? There is infinite speculation on this point. The implications of the Gospels, and the opinion of centuries of Christian tradition (as depicted in the history of art), also has Mary among the disciples at the Ascension of Christ to heaven. Eastern Orthodox churches emphasize Mary's primacy very pointedly, as one of the most important Eastern icons shows the scene of the Ascension of Christ with Mary in the middle of the disciples, her hands upraised.

But the next time we see Mary is in the account in the first two chapters of Acts, as Jesus' remaining followers try to figure out what to do in that upper room. Jesus had promised them that he would send the comforter, the Holy Spirit, to them. As we have seen, Mary was there, and she was also there on the day of Pentecost when "there came a sound like the rush of a violent wind, and it filled the entire house where they were sitting" (Acts 2:2). Once they leave that room, we see and hear no more of Mary in the chronology of the events in the life of Jesus, nor in the chronology of the writings of the New Testament. That is all. But the story, of course, does not end there. For instance, there has been an ancient debate as to whether or not Mary moved to and eventually died in Jerusalem, or Ephesus on the Aegean coast of modern-day Turkey. Even recently, scholars of different persuasions have tried to find the houses that Mary may have lived in after the events of the New Testament were over.

Mary in the middle of the disciples on the day of Pentecost. Detail from a sixth-century Syriac text.

Some have argued that John did as Jesus asked him from the cross and took Mary to live with him in Ephesus. A French abbot from the late nineteenth century, Father Julien Gouyet, is chief among these speculators. He took the mystical visions of Anne Catherine Emmerich (d. 1824) literally in hand (see the next chapter for more on those), as a blueprint for finding Mary's house in Ephesus.

The city of Ephesus played an important role in the development of the Church's teaching and tradition about Mary. In AD 431 Ephesus was the site of the third Church Council of Ephesus, where it was decreed that Mary was to be praised as the *Theotokos*, "Mother of God." It is also fairly certain that Ephesus was indeed the home of St. John sometime soon after the Ascension of Christ. Early church fathers Polycarp (d. 156), Irenaeus (d. 202), and Clement of Alexandria (d. 216) all wrote of John's residing in Ephesus. It was believed that John was, for a time, exiled on the island of Patmos, where he wrote the final book of the Bible, *Revelation*, but that he later returned to Ephesus.

However, just as often, archeologists and other scholars advise that Jerusalem was the place where Mary resided after Christ ascended, and Jerusalem was the place of her death. Speculation has always surrounded the place of Mary's death, and the dogma of her Assumption into heaven soon followed (see chapter eleven), arguing for Jerusalem as her home. One classic, early medieval, apocryphal text, known as *The Book of the Most Holy Virgin, the Mother of God*, or simply, *Pseudo-Melito* (for its author), stated clearly that Mary's Dormition, or "falling asleep" rather than dying, and her rapid Assumption, happened from Jerusalem. In fact, *Pseudo-Melito* depicts each of the Apostles as being raised up by a cloud, amid great confusion, and physically transported to Jerusalem from wherever they happened to be, scattered around the world preaching the gospel. St. John is depicted as coming in this way, from Ephesus. (Theodore the Studite also has Enoch and Elijah arriving from heaven for the event.) They all arrived just before Mary's death, and were said to have witnessed its miracle.

According to local legend, the specific place of the Assumption was in the valley of Josaphat. When Sir John Mandeville wrote about a place for Mary's death in his famous memoirs, *The Travels of Sir John Mandeville*, he apparently did not realize that he was describing the place of her Assumption, not an actual grave:

> Between Jerusalem and the Mount of Olivet is the Valley of Josaphat, below the walls of the city. . . . In the middle of the valley is a church of Our Lady, where her grave is. You must know that when Our Lady died, she was seventy-two years old. Near her grave is the place where Our Lord forgave St. Peter all his sins.

chapter 4

Mary and the Apostle Paul
(Why is he silent?)

Crown him the Virgin's Son,
The God incarnate born,
Whose arm those crimson trophies won
Which now his brow adorn:
Fruit of the mystic Rose,
As of that Rose the Stem;
The Root whence mercy ever flows,
The Babe of Bethlehem.
—Matthew Bridges (d. 1894), from the hymn
"Crown Him with Many Crowns." Mystic
Rose is a metaphor for the Virgin.

*I*N ALL OF THE LETTERS OF PAUL TO THE CHURCHES
that emerged in the first generation of Christianity,
there is only one single reference to Mary. It is, in
fact, a reference that doesn't even name her by name.

But when the fullness of time had come, God sent his
Son, born of a woman, born under the law, in order
to redeem those who were under the law, so that we
might receive adoption as children.

—Galatians 4:4-5

Most scholars agree today that Paul's letters are the oldest documents in the New Testament, and Galatians the oldest among them. Most of the epistles were probably written by Paul to the fledgling Christian communities in the cities of Achaia, Macedonia, Italy, and Asia Minor during the 50s and early 60s, but the letter to the Galatians may have been written as early as 49 or the early 50s. In contrast, the earliest of the four Gospels written was most likely Mark, and dates to approximately twenty years, or a half generation, later. (Many scholars also imagine that there was once a "sayings" gospel, a compilation of the sayings of Jesus, used by Matthew and Luke in compiling their Gospels, and probably written at about the time that Mark was written.)

Why did Paul seem to have nothing to say about Mary in his letters? The answer could be simply that he knew very little about her. Before the four Gospels were created, Paul had already become known as the apostle to the Gentiles, in other words, the first important missionary to non-Jews. While he was alive, Jesus spent most of his time speaking to the Jewish people. Jesus was, of course, a Jew, and the first Christians were also Jews. But immediately after the Resurrection and Ascension, Paul underwent his own con-version on the road to Damascus. This may have happened as early as the mid-30s. And by the time he wrote to the church in Galatia, he had already spent almost fifteen years preaching this new faith to Gentiles. But all of that hap-pened before any of the four Gospels were written. It is very likely that Paul knew little about the Annunciation, the Nativity, the feeding of the five thousand, and other events in the life of Jesus that were brought to life for the Church through the written Gospels. He was martyred in Rome around AD 62, likely before the Gospel of Mark was written.

So, when Paul talks at the beginning of Galatians about "the gospel of Christ," he is not talking about the written

Gospels to come later. He is speaking of the teachings of Christ which were being preached by the disciples throughout Judea and beyond. And throughout the letter, he is primarily concerned to show his readers that the true teaching of Christ is that the Law of the Old Testament has been fulfilled, and no longer is binding on Christians, whether they are Jewish or not. Paul was himself Jewish; in fact, as he says, "I advanced in Judaism beyond many among my people of the same age, for I was far more zealous for the traditions of my ancestors." Nevertheless, he explains that the Jews whom he has converted to the new faith do not need to follow the letter of the old law. They do not, for instance, need to be circumcised or follow Jewish dietary laws (and neither did they have to abandon them). This was a debate that was raging between the original Apostles, particularly among Peter and James, and Paul made his opinion clearly known. The early Church later sided with Paul's interpretation.

Paul preached that a Christian was justified before God by faith in Christ alone, not by the works of the law. He said, "[T]he law was our disciplinarian until Christ came, so that we might be justified by faith. But now that faith has come, we are no longer subject to a disciplinarian" (Galatians 3:24-25). So, when he reminded his readers that Jesus was "born of a woman" Paul was reminding them that the law and prophecies of the Old Testament had been revealed. Jesus was born of a woman, and he was also born under the law in order to fulfill the law by ushering in the era of grace.

Paul probably knew relatively little about the Virgin Mary during the time of his ministry, but also, his theological focus was never on the historical life of Jesus. He instead focused on the meaning of Christ's death and Resurrection. Paul emphasized the redemptive role of the glorified Christ, not the teaching and ministry of the earthly Jesus. He also seems to have deliberately avoided or reversed imagery that later became common references to Mary. For example, in his first letter to the Corinthians, Paul uses the image of milk to refer to the Scriptures, rather than something more maternal. Similarly, in Ephesians chapter five, Paul explains that the Church is Christ's bride, rather than emphasizing the ancient mystical theme from the Song of Songs that symbolized an individual's possible "marriage" to God. And so, since it is in looking at the life of Jesus that we see Mary most clearly, it is no wonder that we see very little of Mary in Paul's letters.

Paul would disagree with those interpreters who later explained that redemption began with the Annunciation to Mary. The events of Jesus' life, teachings, and relationships prior to the Passion were less important to Paul's world-view. For Paul, the seeds of redemption may have been sown when Christ was "born of a woman, born under the law," but it was only really accomplished in the climactic, metaphysical events of his death and Resurrection.

But even though he did not see Mary as the Mother of God, Paul was himself a great mystic. Those Protestants today who look to Paul's emphasis on the risen Christ, more than to the teachings of the earthly Jesus, should realize that the spirit of this approach is almost as profoundly mystical as are the teachings of those Catholics who have given Mary a greater role in salvation history. Paul speaks in wondrous language about the mystical union that is possible with the risen Christ. He instructs the first-century Christians in his various letters how to die in Christ, rise in Christ, fellowship with Christ, belong to Christ, be laid hold of by Christ, put on Christ, and be in Christ. As Albert Schweitzer once explained:

> Thus "in Christ" forms the antithesis to "in the Law."
> . . . The concept of being-in-Christ dominates Paul's

thought in a way that he not only sees in it the source of everything connected with redemption, but describes all the experience, feeling, thought and will of the baptized as taking place in Christ. . . . The fact that the believer's whole being, down to his most ordinary everyday thoughts and actions, is thus brought within the sphere of the mystical experience has its effect of giving to this mysticism a breadth, a permanence, a practicability, and a strength almost unexampled elsewhere in mysticism.[27]

Mary in the Non-Canonical Gospels

And the priest received her, and kissed her,
and blessed her, saying: "The Lord has magnified
thy name in all generations. In thee, on the last of
the days, the Lord will manifest His redemption to
the sons of Israel." And he set her down upon
the third step of the altar, and the Lord God
sent grace upon her; and she danced with her feet,
and all the house of Israel loved her.
—a tale of Mary, age three, from the apocryphal text,
Book of James

*T*HERE ARE MANY NON-CANONICAL GOSPELS OF
Jesus, including the *Gospel of Thomas*, recently
made popular by Dan Brown's novel, *The Da Vinci
Code*; the *Gospel of Philip*; and others. These are often
referred to as Gnostic gospels because they were written and
supported in late antiquity by Gnostic communities that
stood on the fringes of early Christianity.

There are also non-canonical gospels of Mary. It is in
these texts that early Christians first read and developed the

ideas of Mary's holiness and god-likeness. The canonical Gospels do not point us in directions that lead to Mary's Immaculate Conception or Assumption, for instance, but the ancient, non-canonical gospels of Mary, do. These are texts that for various reasons were never included in the New Testament canon, but nevertheless, were known to most of the early Christians who read the rest of the New Testament. In some instances, early church fathers recommended that these texts be included in the canon, but in the end, they were left out.

It is only from these apocryphal texts that we have the traditions of who Mary's parents were (Anne and Joachim), the animals that were present at the Nativity, Mary's lifelong commitment to virginity (modeled as the first nun), and also many tales from Jesus' childhood—many of which are downright frightening.

The first apocryphal infancy gospel of Mary is known as the *Protevangelium*, or, the *Book of James*, and is imagined to be the first ("proto" means first) word on the life of Mary, long before the Annunciation. It was written in the East, most likely Syria, probably two generations after the last of the canonical Gospels (John) was written, and only one generation after the writing of the last New Testament book (2 Peter), in about AD 130. In the *Book of James*, we read many things about Mary that are startling to us, but that were commonly understood by most medieval Christians.

Scholars believe that the author of the *Book of James* was a Jew, and that many of the stories in it originate from the author's desire to challenge first-century Jewish ideas and practices. A vow of virginity, for instance, was alien to Judaism, and the *Book of James* goes to great lengths to demonstrate Mary's commitment to virginity. Also, women were never allowed in the inner court of the Jewish temple, and nowhere near the Holy of Holies, but according to this text, Mary played there as a child. The author of the *Book of James* portrays Mary growing up, from age three to sixteen, in the temple, as she is cared for by the high priest himself. Jacobus de Voragine's *The Golden Legend* adds: "Angels visited her every day, and she enjoyed the vision of God daily." According to Jacobus, Mary even prepared a monastic rule for herself, and lived by it. The Annunciation itself is pinpointed to have happened when Mary was sixteen.

Another startling feature of this ancient, apocryphal text is that Mary does not fully explain herself to Joseph, or again to the high priest, when questioned as to how she came to be pregnant. In both stories, when she is confronted, the text reads that Mary "wept bitterly" and explains that she is pure, and has never had sexual relations with any man. But, she doesn't repeat what the archangel so clearly said to her at the Annunciation: "That holy thing which shall be born of thee shall be called the Son of the Most High. And thou shalt call His name Jesus, for He shall save His people from their sins." For some reason, she keeps that part to herself.

Finally, in the *Book of James*, that last phrase of the archangel's message—"He shall save His people from their sins"—is announced to Mary at the Annunciation, when, in the New Testament, we don't hear about Jesus saving anyone's sins until John the Baptist announces in John's Gospel, "Here is the Lamb of God who takes away the sin of the world!" For the medieval imagination, this was further proof that Mary knew the full range of God's plans for salvation, even before her son was born.

THE GOSPEL OF THE BIRTH OF MARY

Eventually, by the eighth or ninth century, the *Book of James* and other texts were combined together and translated into Latin, the vernacular language of the West. These stories were so pervasive to the myth of Mary that the medieval understanding of her would be completely lost to us, today, if it were not for that Latin text which came to be known as *The Gospel of the Birth of Mary*. Sometimes called *The Gospel of Pseudo-Matthew*, after the legend that the disciple, Matthew, wrote it, it was believed that St. Jerome translated the text into Latin, and it has a prologue that bears his name. *The Golden Legend* credits Jerome as the author of *The Gospel of the Birth of Mary*, but most scholars today doubt that claim.

In any case, it is from *The Gospel of the Birth of Mary*, as well as the *Book of James* that preceded it, that the Middle Ages came to "know" many things about Mary that are not included in the New Testament. Some of it rings true to a modern ear, and much of it does not. For instance, chapter one describes Joachim, Mary's father, as saying: "there was no man like him in the people of Israel."[28] This seems like a classic instance of hagiographic storytelling, in which a writer will import some detail from a foundational life of a previous prophet in order to create a similar impression and support for a new story. Joachim is described like Abram, whose name means "exalted ancestor," and like Job, who was "blameless and upright."

Other details of *The Gospel of the Birth of Mary* ring true, however. In chapter two, when Joachim arrives at the temple during a time of feast to offer his gifts of incense, he is spurned by the priest. The priest humiliates him, saying: "You should not stand here where men have come to offer sacrifice to God because God has not blessed you with children for Israel." The text reads that Joachim was "put to shame in the sight of the people," and why wouldn't he be! So, he left, traveling a thirty-day distance from home, sulking and ashamed, and away from his wife, Anne.

It was precisely at that time, while Joachim was away, that the text describes an angel coming to Anne with news about her being with child, just as the angel later came to her daughter, Mary, in the Annunciation. The angel then goes to Joachim in the mountains where he is hiding away, feeling sorry for himself, and tells him the news, as well.

The similarities between this non-canonical life of the Virgin Mary and the New Testament Gospels become more acute in chapter four. We cannot, in fact, understand the scene in Luke of Jesus as a boy in the temple in Jerusalem—staying behind, against his parents' wishes—as medieval Christians understood it, unless we see what is written in *The Gospel of the Birth of Mary*. When Mary was only three years old, *The Gospel of the Birth of Mary* reads, Anne and Joachim took Mary with them to the temple in order to offer sacrifices. The child Mary took to the temple without doubt or hesitancy, mounting the stairs with great excitement.

> And when [Mary] was put down before the doors of the temple, she went up the fifteen steps so swiftly, that she did not look back at all; nor did she, as children are wont to do, seek for her parents. Whereupon her parents, each of them anxiously seeking for the child, were both alike astonished, until they found her in the temple, and the priests of the temple themselves wondered.

In the Accademia delle Belle Arti in Venice may be found a lovely painting by Titian entitled "Presentation of the Virgin in the Temple." Light shines from the young girl's body, as she ascends the stairs to the temple, approaching the bearded high priest, whose arms are rising to greet her. People are leaning out of windows to glimpse her, and peasants below look dumbfounded at her boldness.

This story—commonly understood by Christians up until the time of the Reformation, explains why Mary is often shown with a book on her lap at the moment of the Annunciation. In Fra Angelico's painting "The Annunciation," for instance, Mary is sitting in a portico with a book on her lap, reading, when the archangel Gabriel arrives with his heavenly message. She wasn't working in the house, or sleeping, or talking with her parents or friends—she was studying. There are many popular images of Mary at study, throughout history.

Mary was given by her parents to the temple priests as a young girl. She lived with the virgins of the temple until such time as a proper husband would later be found for her. But Mary later resisted these attempts to wed her, and in so doing, created the first movement of nuns. Chapter seven of *The Gospel of the Birth of Mary* explains that she vowed from young womanhood never to wed or be with a man. This was in response to a request from the high priest that Mary wed his own son. The text has Mary teaching the high priest: "God is worshiped in chastity." Again, the text reads that the high priest, after having learned from Mary's words and example, rose and said to all of the people gathered there: "A new order of life has been found out by Mary alone, who promises that she will remain a virgin to God. Wherefore it seems to me, that through our inquiry and the answer of God we should try to ascertain to whose keeping she ought to be entrusted." Apparently, a lifelong virgin needs a man to take care of her, and eventually Joseph is found, again by angelic intervention, and he is described as an old man who already has grandchildren that are older than Mary. "I shall be her guardian," Joseph says, and Mary is brought to his house along with five other virgins as companions.

MARY IN ISLAM

"The angels cast lots with arrows (like cupids), as to which of them should be charged with the care of Mary."
—Qur'an, 3:44

The Gospel of the Birth of Mary was so common and accepted in the Middle Ages that some of these additions to her legend were even repeated in Islam's Holy Scripture, the Qur'an. The Qur'an is made up of 114 suras, or chapters, each containing many verses. Suras 3 and 19 have much to do with Mary, showing how she is revered in Islam, as is her son. No other woman is discussed as much as Mary is, in the Qur'an. Sura 3 is titled "The Family of Imran, The House of Imran" in one of the oldest and most respected English translations (*The Meanings Of The Holy Qur'an*, by Abdullah Yusufali), which I have contemporized only slightly, below. In this long selection, many of the traditions from *The Gospel of the Birth of Mary* are picked up: Mary's mother Anne and her prayers to God for a child; Anne's gift of her only daughter to the Lord; God's predestination of Mary as innocent, pure, and set apart. In addition, sura 3, verse 44 adds the most charming addition of all to the legend of the infancy of Mary. "The angels cast lots with arrows (like cupids), as to which of them should be charged with the care of Mary." (see below) Also, the priest in the temple—to whom young Mary is given for raising and keeping pure—turns out to be the same Zachariah, the priest who is also the father of John the Baptist.

[33.]Allah did choose Adam and Noah, the family of Abraham, and the family of Imran (Joachim, in Christian tradition) above all people—

[34.]Offspring, one of the other: And Allah hears and knows all things.

[35.]Behold! a woman of Imran [this is Anne, in Christian tradition] said: "O my Lord! I do dedicate to Thee what is in my womb for Thy special service: So accept this of me: For Thou hears and knows all things."

[36.]When she was delivered, she said: "O my Lord! Behold! I am delivered of a female child!" and Allah knew best what she brought forth. [Anne is disappointed that her child, because she is a girl, will not be a scholar or priest, but Allah knows better. . . .] "And no wise is the male like the female. I have named her Mary, and I commend her and her offspring to Thy protection from the Evil One, the Rejected."

[37.]Right graciously did her Lord accept her: He made her grow in purity and beauty: To the care of Zakariya [Zachariah, a priest in the temple] was she assigned. Every time that he entered her chamber to see her, he found her supplied with sustenance. He said: "O Mary! From where did this come?" She said: "From Allah for Allah provides sustenance to whom He pleases without measure." [In what follows, we see that the child, Mary, is the teacher of the elderly priest, Zachariah.]

^{38.}There did Zakariya pray to his Lord, saying: "O my Lord! Grant unto me from Thee a progeny that is pure: for Thou art He that hears prayer!" [Zachariah turns out to be the same Zachariah who was married to Elizabeth, the mother of John the Baptist.]

^{39.}While he was standing in prayer in the chamber, the angels called unto him: "Allah gives thee glad tidings of Yahya [John the Baptist], witnessing the truth of a Word from Allah, and be besides noble, chaste, and a prophet—of the good company of the righteous."

^{41.}He said: "O my Lord! Give me a Sign!" "Thy Sign," was the answer, "shall be that thou shall speak to no man for three days but with signals. Then celebrate the praises of thy Lord again and again, and glorify Him in the evening and in the morning."

^{42.}"Behold!" the angels said. "O Mary! Allah has chosen thee and purified thee—chosen thee above the women of all nations."

^{43.}"Mary, worship Thy Lord devoutly: Prostrate thyself, and bow down in prayer with those who bow down."

^{44.}This is part of the tidings of the things unseen, which we reveal unto thee (O Messenger) by inspiration: Thou was not with them when they cast lots with arrows, as to which of them should be charged with the care of Mary. Nor was thou with them when they disputed the point.

^{45.}"Behold!" the angels said. "Mary, Allah gives thee glad tidings of a Word from Him: his name will be Christ Jesus, the son of Mary, held in honor in this world and the hereafter and of the company of those nearest to Allah."

46."He shall speak to the people in childhood and in maturity. And he shall be of the company of the righteous."

47.Mary said: "O my Lord! How shall I have a son when no man hath touched me?" He said: "Even so: Allah creates what He wills. When He has decreed a plan, He but says to it, 'Be,' and it is!"

It is remarkable how much of both the canonical and non-canonical gospels are repeated in this sura from the Qur'an. Islam accepts the notion of the Immaculate Conception of Mary (discussed in more detail in chapter 11), and also accepts much of the Gospel accounts about the virgin birth, but it differs primarily on the nature of the child, Jesus. The Qur'an insists that Jesus was not God, but a prophet to be revered. In this sense, the virgin birth of Christ is compared to the origin of Adam, who was born without father or mother.

Other Islamic texts, particularly those written by Sufis, the mystical branch of Islam, offer additional details relating to the Annunciation. Sufism has always been interested in the presences of angels, and the great Sufi poet Rumi offers this expansion of the story of the Annunciation, even before the archangel Gabriel said a single word.

Mary, being privately in her chamber, beheld a life-augmenting, heart-ravishing form: the Trusty Spirit rose up before her from the face of the earth, bright as the moon and the sun. Beauty without a veil rose up from the earth, even like as the sun rising in splendor from the East. Trembling overcame Mary's limbs, for she was naked and feared corruption. Mary became unselfed, and in her selflessness she cried, "I will leap into the Divine protection."[29]

Mary in the Non-Canonical Gospels

Another tale from Rumi, like a good Jewish midrash, adds to the story of Mary and Elizabeth's greeting each other, each of them pregnant to their delight and surprise, Mary with Christ, Elizabeth with John the Baptist. The first chapter of the Gospel of Luke tells the story, "When Elizabeth heard Mary's greeting, the child leaped in her womb" (1:41), and Rumi adds another salutation, from Christ to John:

> Once, while she was pregnant, the mother of John found Mary, also with child, sitting before her. She told Mary that she perceived within Mary's womb "a king," who was to be a prophet of the first rank, and that she felt the child within her own womb bowing and prostrating himself in deference to the child in Mary's, and that all this was causing her terrible trial and pain. Jesus, Mary replied, was doing the same prostrations in her womb.[30]

Sura 3 of the Qur'an concludes this section on Mary and Jesus by describing what the boy will grow up to do. Jesus is predestined to be an apostle (or a "prophet" in most translations) to Israel. He is one of Allah's messengers and helpers, as was Mary his mother, which makes both of them good Muslims in Islamic tradition.

48."And Allah will teach him the Book and Wisdom, the Law and the Gospel,

49."And appoint him an apostle to the Children of Israel, with this message: 'I have come to you, with a Sign from your Lord, in that I make for you out of clay, as it were, the figure of a bird, and breathe into it, and it becomes a bird by Allah's leave. And I heal those born blind, and the lepers, and I quicken the dead, by Allah's leave; and I declare to you what you eat, and what you store in your houses. Surely there is a Sign for you if you did believe;

[50.]'I have come to you to attest the Law which was before me. And to make lawful to you part of what was before forbidden to you; I have come to you with a Sign from your Lord. So fear Allah, and obey me.

[51.]'It is Allah Who is my Lord and your Lord; then worship Him. This is a Way that is straight.'

[52.]"When Jesus found unbelief on their part He said: 'Who will be My helpers to the work of Allah.' Said the disciples: 'We are Allah's helpers: We believe in Allah, and do therefore bear witness that we are Muslims.'"

Sura 19 of the Qur'an, meanwhile, is titled "Mary" or "Miriam" (Arabic for "Mary") and offers additional information about her, building on what was said in sura 3. Mary and Jesus are both affirmed as prophets, and Mary repeats the famous phrase from the New Testament: "He has made me blessed."

Most important, the Qur'an shows a picture of Mary doing what her primary task is to do: pointing people to her son. Islam expands our understanding of Mary as a prophet by adding this detail to the infancy narratives of Christ in the New Testament. In verse 29, Mary resolutely points to the baby when all of the attention is being heaped upon her. She is so devoted to spreading the news of who he is and who he is to become that her people are left asking, "How can we talk to a baby?" And to their great surprise—and to ours!—he talks!

[27.]At length she brought the babe to her people, carrying him in her arms. They said: "O Mary! truly an amazing thing has thou brought!

^{28.}"O sister of Aaron! Thy father was not a man of evil, nor thy mother a woman unchaste!"

^{29.}But she pointed to the babe. They said: "How can we talk to one who is a child in the cradle?"

^{30.}He said: "I am indeed a servant of Allah. He has given me revelation and made me a prophet;

^{31.}"And He has made me blessed wherever I be, and has enjoined on me Prayer and Charity as long as I live;

^{32.}"He has made me kind to my mother, and not overbearing or miserable;

^{33.}"So peace is on me the day I was born, the day that I die, and the day that I shall be raised up to life again!"

^{34.}Such was Jesus the son of Mary. It is a statement of truth about which they vainly dispute.

^{35.}It is not befitting to the majesty of Allah that He should beget a son. Glory be to Him! When He determines a matter, He only says to it, "Be," and it is.

Finally, notice how the Qur'an, in its overriding respect for Mary, offers a story to help explain the Gospel account that suggests Jesus may have been dismissing his mother's concern for him, while he was lingering and teaching in the temple. In the quote above, Jesus himself explains from sura 19: "I am indeed a servant of God. He hath given me revelation and made me a prophet, and He hath made me blessed wherever I be." The prophet is a good son, and a good son has his reward: "He hath made me kind to my mother, and not overbearing or unblessed. So, peace is on me the day I was born, the day that I die, and the day that I shall be raised up to life again!"

Strange Heaven

HOLY ANTECEDENTS:
FROM CHRIST TO MARY TO ANNE

The ancient Church in both the East and the West began celebrating Mary's birth no later than the seventh century. She was believed to have been born in Jerusalem on the eighth of September. But that wasn't enough for the early Christians who were devoted to her. Naturally, Mary must have been conceived approximately nine months prior to September 8, and so the eighth of December became another feast for Mary. In the Western church, this was known as the Feast of the Immaculate Conception of Mary, while in the East it was simply the Conception of St. Anne (her mother).

Many other church feasts arose to celebrate the non-canonical devotions to the "Holy Infant Mary." These are ways of honoring Mary who heralded Jesus, but also Anne who heralded Mary. Like her son, Mary was also believed to have been "presented" in the temple in Jerusalem by Anne and Joachim. This was said to have happened on November 21. In some parts of the world, observing these feasts is an important part of devotion to the infancy and girlhood of Mary. In Mexico City, for instance, these devotions are strong today. They are fueled by a local tradition that says Mary appeared to a young nun, Sister Magdalena, as she knelt before a nativity scene on January 6, 1840. The sister reported seeing a beautiful young girl appear before her saying, "I will grant great graces to whoever honors me in my infancy." Many statues have been made—modeled after the one that Sister Magdalena first commissioned—and are venerated throughout the country.

All of this troubles some Christians. We struggle with the ancient beliefs in Mary as an intercessor to Christ, but then, if devotions are added to Mary as a child and also to Mary's mother, it is natural to ask: Where will it stop?

Mary in the Non-Canonical Gospels

Of the many popular prayer cards that are available at most any Catholic book or gift shop, I find the images of Mary's mother, Anne, most interesting. She is often rendered like a Sunday school teacher, instructing the young girl (Mary) seated before her, who is all rapt with attention, in the ways of piety. There is always a halo around Anne's head—which is of course typical, since these are prayer cards of saints—but the young Mary sometimes does not wear one; she has not yet been visited by the archangel.

The prayers that appear on the back of these cards are usually worded for the obtaining of some favor. On St. Anne cards, the prayer goes, in part, something like this:

Glorious St. Anne, filled with compassion for those who come to thee, and with love for all who suffer, recommend my special request to thy Daughter, the Blessed Virgin Mary, laying it before the throne of Jesus. Good St. Anne, mother of her who is our Life, Sweetness, and Hope, pray to your Daughter for me and help me to obtain my request.

From our hearts to Anne's ears, then to Mary, and on to Christ. These many layers of petitionary prayer were common in the Middle Ages and still are—among the most traditional of Catholic devotions—today. In Dante's fourteenth-century epic poem, *The Divine Comedy*, Bernard of Clairvaux is quoted as saying that Anne's role in the heavenly kingdom is next to that of St. Peter:

Opposite Peter seest thou Anne seated,
So well content to look upon her daughter,
Her eyes she moves not while she sings Hosanna.
(Canto XXXII)

Strange Heaven

Many popular statues were created throughout the Middle Ages, called *Anna Selbdritts* in German, depicting Anne as the throne for both Mary and her son, Jesus. Anne was seen, and venerated as, the throne and womb of salvation. Just as Mary was the Mother of God and of Christian redemption, Anne was regarded as the root of it all—the root from which salvation grew. One popular medieval poem said: "Hail fortunate Anne parent of the Virgin Mary / Worthily you laid the warp of the work of our salvation."[31]

Most fantastically, legend also had it that Anne married three times, and that she was ultimately responsible for not only Mary and Jesus, but for several of the first apostles and disciples of Christ. She first married Joachim, as we saw above in *The Gospel of the Birth of Mary*, and gave birth to the Virgin Mary, who later gave birth to Jesus. Next, she married Cleophas and gave birth to Mary Cleophas; this Mary gave birth to James the Lesser, Jude Thaddeus, Simon, and Joseph the Just (the one who was runner up to Matthias in becoming the replacement apostle for Judas, after the Crucifixion). Finally, according to this popular legend, Anne married Salome and gave birth to yet another Mary, Mary Salome. Mary Salome later mothered James the Greater and John the Beloved.

Anne (mother of many)

Husband	Joachim	Cleophas	Salome
Child	The Virgin Mary	Mary Cleophas	Mary Salome
Grandchildren	Jesus Christ	James the Lesser	James the Greater
		Jude Thaddeus	John the Beloved

Catholic tradition has held Anne—Mary's legendary mother—in high esteem indeed. It is as if the pious were not to be satisfied, first with Christ, then with the special role played by Mary, so they finally had to appeal to Anne. In these non-canonical traditions, both Anne and her more-famous daughter were objects of veneration, the greatest of the saints, and important pathways to God's ear.

CHAPTER 6

Mystical Glosses that Further
Added to the Myth

I had a vision of the creation of Mary's most holy
soul and of its being united to her most pure body.
In the glory by which the Most Holy Trinity is usually
represented in my visions I saw a movement like a
great shining mountain, and yet also like a human
figure; and I saw something rise out of the midst
of this figure towards its mouth and go forth from
it like a shining brightness. Then I saw this brightness standing separate before the Face of God,
turning and shaping itself—or rather being
shaped, for I saw that while this brightness took
human form, yet it was by the Will of God that it
received a form so unspeakably beautiful. . . . I am
unable to describe in words all that I saw and
understood.

—Anne Catherine Emmerich, from her visions
entitled *The Life of the Blessed Virgin Mary*

URING THE FIRST CENTURY OF CHRISTIANITY,
from approximately AD 50 onward, the writings were composed that later became the
canonical New Testament. In the second century, from
about AD 135 onward, many other books were written
about the life and teachings of Christ and of Mary. These

were often circulated widely and read by the same early Christians who were schooled in the Gospels of Matthew, Mark, Luke, and John, and the writings of St. Paul. By the time of the first churchwide Council of Nicaea, in 325, the canon was firmly set. But both during and after Nicaea, there appears to have been little hesitancy among the faithful to accept ideas and traditions that remained outside of the official canon. Perhaps the feeling was that this new movement was still being revealed, but in addition to that, it was also being interpreted in lively ways.

Some of these texts were discussed in the last chapter. In addition, the Middle Ages saw the growth of various mystical glosses or commentaries that built on the early legends of Mary. These were not documents that attempted to *be* gospels, but they were nevertheless believed to be true. In many cases, they are written more like mystical novels. They are often recordings of visions believed by mystics to have been given to them by Christ, telling of feelings, motivations, and actions about which the biblical accounts remained silent. In these remarkable testaments, Mary becomes a goddess, a visionary, and nearly omniscient.

THE GODDESS

Any reader of the Old Testament knows that goddess traditions were alive and well throughout Palestine, Asia Minor, and in other parts of the Egyptian, Babylonian, and Sumerian kingdoms of the three millennia before Christ. The Israelites were often tempted to worship pagan gods and sometimes did so. Ezekiel speaks of women "weeping for Tammuz" at the entrance of the house of the Lord. Other Hebrew prophets, such as Daniel, Isaiah, and Hosea, denounced gods and goddesses without naming them. The worship of these goddess cults, many of them the sort of nature-worship that we sometimes see today, was denounced by the Hebrew prophets and then again by the early Christians. But nevertheless, the understanding of how these goddesses offer a motherly sort of spiritual guidance most likely became, consciously or unconsciously, a guide for the early Christian legends surrounding Mary and her powers.

Churches were often built and dedicated to Mary in cities like Ephesus, on top of destroyed temples to ancient goddesses. The Christian conversion of the Roman Emperor Constantine hastened these transitions in the fourth and fifth centuries. Many of the miracles that are credited to Mary in the early, mystical texts about her may be traced back to goddess legends. Sally Cunneen offers one example, showing Mary's goddess like ability to influence the growth of crops:

> One example is the legend that added a grain miracle to the Virgin's activities during the Flight into Egypt. When Mary passed by a farmer's field, the story goes, she graciously offered to help him raise an instant crop. In that way he would not have to lie to the soldiers when they asked if Mary had passed by recently. "Just when I planted this field," he could say.[32]

Religion rarely ever begins things. It refashions them, renews them, re-interprets them, redeems them. The Christmas celebration of today, and even the dating of Christmas as December 25, began as an alternative to pagan winter solstice celebrations. The modern hymn began in the tavern, with tunes of merry-making. Holy fools wouldn't make sense without a dominant culture to rebel against. Telling the stories of saints' lives began as a healthy alternative to those of the gods and heroes of popular mythology. Even so, some of the earliest theologians of the Church gave sermons and wrote treatises to denounce the mingling of goddess worship and reverence for Mary. It was common to confuse the two.

But while many of the early Christian theologians were worried that borrowing on goddess traditions would taint Mary with paganism, more recently, and for very different reasons, feminist scholars have also wished that these mystical texts would have left the goddess traditions alone. Beginning sixty years ago with the French existentialist Simone de Beauvoir, these writers have lamented the Church's usurping of the power of goddess traditions for the subservience of the Virgin Mary. For example, wrote de Beauvoir, when Luke has Mary announcing herself to be the *handmaid* of the Lord, "For the first time in the history of mankind a mother kneels before her son and acknowledges, of her own free will, her inferiority. The supreme victory of masculinity is consummated in Mariolatry: it signifies the rehabilitation of woman through the completeness of her defeat."

More recently, the controversial Boston College professor Mary Daly said in her book *Beyond God the Father* that the concept of Mary, as developed in the New Testament texts, is a "pale derivative symbol disguising the conquered Goddess." Where the ancient goddess had power, Mary gives up her power. Where the goddess was all-knowing, Mary looks to her son.

THE VISIONARY

But Mary remains, if not all-knowing, a woman of remarkable vision.

The dictum of the Protestant Reformation as to what makes for religious truth did not exist before the sixteenth century. In other words, the notion that, in order for a religious statement to be true it must be verifiable in the Bible, did not exist. Many of the first Protestants used this measure as a way of eradicating beliefs that had become dangerous, such as: "Money paid to the Church in honor of a saint will release your loved one from purgatory and send him/her directly to heaven." Similarly, other early Protestants used this dictum to declare that all statuary of Mary, hymn-books, and other religious articles should be stripped from the churches because the Bible does not make mention of them.

Both before and after the Reformation, the Catholic imagination has insisted on a more expansive view of what is true. The Catholic imagination allows for God to speak privately to individuals, and for those messages to become widely believed, without the necessity of deciding their level of truth for the body as a whole. There are beliefs that are good but not necessarily true, and they are good simply because they produce good effects.

The legends of the saints are full of these ideas and traditions. Mary's role as visionary was created, in large part, by these mystical glosses on the biblical tradition. For example, *The Golden Legend* says this about Mary, adding to the biblical role that she played after Christ's Passion:

> The third apparition [of the resurrected Christ on Easter Day] was to the Virgin Mary and is believed to have taken place before all the others, although the evangelists say nothing about it. . . . [I]f this is not to be believed, on the ground that no evangelist testifies to it . . . perish the thought that such a son would fail to honor such a mother by being so negligent! . . . Christ must first of all have made his mother happy over his resurrection, since she certainly grieved over

his death more than the others. He would not have neglected his mother while he hastened to console others.

For medieval Christians, Mary was the most important person at the cross, the tomb, in the Upper Room, and at the Ascension. The various biblical accounts offer some small support for these ideas—or, at least, for the idea that Mary was in each of these places—but the best reason for the belief in Mary's primacy was simply that it made spiritual sense. In the way in which the medieval imagination "knew" Mary, it made good sense to believe that her wisdom, compassion, and patience were in some way guiding the events on earth around the aftermath of her son's death and Resurrection.

The Virgin is portrayed in Catholic tradition as one who knew how to measure the length and breadth of salvation history. Once the archangel Gabriel brought the Annunciation to Mary, tradition has given her all manners of foreknowledge. Father Alban Butler, for instance, wrote 250 years ago in his famous *Lives of the Saints* about the circumcision of our Lord (celebrated on January 1), comparing that very small suffering to the greater suffering that was to come. And Mary apparently knew it all from the beginning.

> With what sentiments did Mary bear in her womb, bring forth, and serve her adorable son, who was also her God? With what love and awe did she fix her eyes upon him, particularly at his circumcision, who can express in what manner she was affected when she saw him subjected to this painful and humbling ceremony? . . . In amorous complaints that he would begin, in the excess of his love, to suffer for us in so tender an age, and to give this earnest of our redemption, she might say to him: "Truly you are a bridegroom of blood to

me" (Exodus 4:25). With the early sacrifice Christ here made of himself to his Father, she joined her own, offering her divine son, and with and through him herself, to be an eternal victim to his honor and love, with the most ardent desire to suffer all things, even to blood, for the accomplishment of his will.

It was Christ's suffering, in fact, that almost always filled Mary's foreknowledge. The Gospel of Luke itself offers evidence that Mary knew her son was headed for suffering from his childhood. When she and Joseph brought Jesus to the temple, they met old Simeon who told Mary, "This child is destined for the falling and the rising of many in Israel, and to be a sign that will be opposed so that the inner thoughts of many will be revealed—and a sword will pierce your own soul too." Tradition has it that the fourth Station of the Cross, known as "Jesus Meets His Blessed Mother" (while carrying his cross to Calvary) was a fulfillment of Simeon's prophecy.

ALL-KNOWING MARY

The tradition of mystical commentaries about Mary, each expanding her role from what is known in the Gospels, continues today. These texts are like Jewish midrash, in that they tell stories that purport to "fill in the gaps" of what we don't see or hear in the New Testament. In the last two centuries, perhaps the most influential glosses of Mary have come from the Augustinian nun Anne Catherine Emmerich (d. 1824). Her visions, or meditations, were recorded in various books including *The Life of the Blessed Virgin Mary* (quoted at the beginning of this chapter), and *The Dolorous Passion of Our Lord Jesus Christ*.[33] These books were first written in German and then translated into many languages. They have remained in print for almost two centuries, but briefly became a sensation when Mel Gibson used many of Emmerich's ideas for the screenplay to his controversial blockbuster film, *The Passion of the Christ* (2004). The narrative that Emmerich creates is completely medieval in its vision of evil pervading everyday life, and its notions of how evil may be easily diagnosed in human behavior.

In *The Dolorous Passion of Our Lord Jesus Christ*, the mystic's interpretations on the sketchy events of the Passion are divided into nine meditations entitled "Preparations for the Passover," followed by sixty-six chapters on the Passion itself. All together, these recorded visions read like a horribly anti-Semitic novelist's creative expansion of what little is known from the Gospels. She had the mind of a film director in the way she "saw" the events of the Passion play themselves out in fine and dramatic detail. She watches the Virgin as she, in turn, watches her son experience all of the humiliation and pain of the Passion and the Crucifixion. Mary follows him, as mother and as disciple, resolutely joining him in his suffering.

Emmerich claims to have seen many things, some clearly and some not so clearly, but all in visions as if she is watch-

ing a story unfold. She makes many connections between the events of the last days of Jesus and the characters and events of the Hebrew Bible. Some of these connections come across as completely preposterous. She sees, for instance, that the chalice used by Christ at the Last Supper was previously owned by Abraham and also by Noah; it had, in fact, "been preserved in Noah's Ark," she opines (Meditation IV).

But the relationship between mother and son is deep and intimate in Emmerich's visions, and movingly so. As Jesus was going up to Jerusalem for Passover, when he "announced to his Blessed Mother what was going to take place, she besought him, in the most touching terms, to let her die with him. But he exhorted her to show more calmness in her sorrow than the other women. . . . She did not weep much, but . . . there was something almost awful in her look of deep recollection" (Meditation V). Many of the reviews of Gibson's movie, even those that were critical of it as being excessively violent and perpetuating of anti-Semitic attitudes, recommended the poignant and multi-faceted portrayal of the Mother of Jesus. Gibson borrowed all of these ideas from Anne Catherine Emmerich.

In contrast to St. Ambrose, who argued in the fifth century that Mary would never have cried for Christ during the Passion or at the foot of the cross simply because she knew the broad sweep of God's salvation plans, Emmerich stands in the parallel, medieval tradition that paints a different picture. While Jesus was in the Garden of Gethsemane, set upon by all the evil in the world for which he was about to die, Anne Catherine recounts: "During this agony of Jesus, I saw the Blessed Virgin also overwhelmed with sorrow and anguish of soul, in the house of Mary, the mother of Mark. She was with Magdalene and Mary in the garden belonging to the house . . ." (Chapter I). The parallel storyline of the Passion of Jesus and the whereabouts and experiences of the Virgin, continues. "The Blessed Virgin was ever united to her Divine Son by interior spiritual communications. . . . [She] ever beheld in spirit the opprobrious treatment which her dear Son was receiving." (Chapter XI). The all-knowing Mary is also the all-suffering mother.

Mary becomes the first person to practice the Stations of the Cross—a Christian's exemplar in replicating the sorrow and pain of Christ as a path to deeper understanding of the release from sin. "When Jesus was taken before Herod, John led the Blessed Virgin and Magdalene over the parts which had been sanctified by his footsteps. . . . [T]hey stopped and contemplated each spot where he had fallen, or where he had suffered particularly. . . . The Blessed Virgin knelt down frequently and kissed the ground where her Son had fallen. . . . [T]hus were the Mysteries of the Passion of Jesus first honored, even before that Passion was accomplished" (Chapter XVIII).

The picture painted of the role of Mary during the Passion is definitely profound. Mary's spiritual experience becomes the archetype for we who follow her. She is portrayed clearly as the first of the Apostles. Foreshadowing symbolism and subtle connections are everywhere in Anne Catherine's narrative. "When Jesus fell down at the foot of the pillar, after the flagellation, I saw Claudia Procles, the wife of Pilate, send some large pieces of linen to the Mother of God. I know not whether she thought that Jesus would be set free, and that his Mother would then require linen to dress his wounds, or whether this compassionate lady was aware of the use which would be made of her present" (Chapter XXIII).

But the original emphasis on the sorrows of the Virgin predates Emmerich by several hundred years. St. Bridget of Sweden (d. 1373), for instance, wrote of many visions in which both Mary and Christ told her of the events—and their inner anguish and pain—during the Passion. In one passage, she recounts what Mary told her about the time of the scourging of Jesus: "And then he was violently thrown to the ground and his head struck the ground so hard that his teeth knocked together. And they struck him so pitilessly on the face and neck that although I was not standing close I could hear it. . . . The first blow struck my heart so painfully that I fainted. When I came to myself again I saw that his body was torn all over."[34] It is from images such as these that Mary was revered as the *Mater Dolorosa*, or "Suffering Mother." She not only mourned the suffering of her son, and physically identified with it as any good parent might, but Mary also suffered herself, in a mystical identification with the suffering that was necessary in order to bring about human redemption. At its most extreme, the *Mater Dolorosa* is pictured with a sword piercing her breast, sometimes even seven swords piercing her breast, as she experienced each of the seven sorrows associated with Christ's passion.

Similarly, many medieval commentators expanded on the scene recounted in John chapter nineteen (and curiously only in John's Gospel, not the other three) of Mary standing vigil at the foot of the cross. From this brief mention in the

last of the Gospels emerged the powerful, extra-biblical image known as the *Pietà*—sculpted and painted by many artists—when the dead Christ is put into his mother's sorrowful arms. There is no known precedent for the *Pietà* in other religious or mythic traditions, and it is not an image that arises from the biblical accounts. However, its power speaks to every parent, particularly to parents who have had to endure the loss of a child, especially the loss of a child who was a victim of violence. Additional traditions have Mary supporting the head of Jesus as it was carried to the cave of Joseph of Arimathea for burial.

Despite her foreknowledge of her son's suffering, throughout the Middle Ages Mary's role as *Mater Dolorosa* increased. The remarkable poem, *Stabat Mater Dolorosa*, was written by the Franciscan friar Jacopone da Todi in the fourteenth century. It is essential for the poem, and for the legend, that the Virgin Mother is not just suffering, but she is standing—a witness to the events. Mary transforms suffering through her courage and witness, just as her son transformed it through the accomplishment of God's will. In English, the poem runs like this:

The grieving mother stood weeping, beside the cross her station keeping on which her Son was hanging;

Who trembled, grieved, bosom heaving, while perceiving, scarcely believing, the torment of her glorious son.

Through her weeping soul, sorrowing and agonizing, a cruel sword passed.

What man would not weep, when seeing Christ's mother in such sadness and grief?

O how mournful and afflicted was that blessed mother of the only son,

Who could not but have compassion witnessing that mother tender suffering with her child?

Mystical Glosses that Further Added to the Myth

For the sins of his people atoning, she saw Jesus in torment groaning, given to the scourger's rod.

She saw her sweet offspring dying, desolate, forsaken, crying yield his spirit up to God.

Mary, make me feel thy sorrow's power, that with thee I tears may shower, tender mother, fount of love!

Make my heart with love unceasing burn toward Christ the Lord, pleasing may I be to him above.

Holy mother, if this be granted, that the slain one's wounds be planted firmly in my heart to bide,

Of him wounded, all astounded—depths unbounded for me sounded—and all the pangs with me divide.

Make me weep with thee in union; with the Crucified, communion in his grief and suffering give;

Near the cross, with tears unfailing, I would join thee in thy wailing here as long as I shall live.

Maid of maidens, all excelling! be not bitter, me repelling; make me a mourner too.

Make me bear about Christ's dying, share his passion, shame defying, all his wounds in me renew.

Wound for wound create in me, with the cross intoxicated for thy Son's dear sake, I pray.

May I, fired with pure affection, have your protection in the solemn Judgment Day.

Let me by the cross be warded, by the death of Christ be guarded, nourished by divine supplies.

When the body's death has riven, grant that to my soul be given glories bright of Paradise.[35]

Despite the medieval glorification of human suffering in these mystical commentaries, these texts also offer renewed understandings of the meaning of life, death, and eternity. Christians sometimes forget that Christianity has always taught the permeability of the boundary between life and death. We call death "after-life" for a reason. The empty tomb is the prime image of what it means to be Christian—not the suffering of Jesus on the cross. We can comprehend human suffering better than we can imagine resurrections from death, but that shouldn't stop us from knowing the essence of what it means to be Christian. We are living in eternity, even in the midst of the suffering of daily life. Life and death are one; together, they are events on a longer course.

The Blessed Virgin Mary
in Catholicism

"**M**ARY WAS MYSTERIOUS, AND THEREFORE for Catholics; our [Protestant] religion was more proper, more masculine."

—Kathleen Norris[36]

Appearing Now in a Field Near You (Apparitions and Visions)

"Mary is . . . in the process of writing her own story and revealing her own convictions and wisdom as she has appeared in people's lives since the Gospels were written. The threads of these sightings make up centuries of tales about an active presence over time who longs for the human family to live together in peace and love, whole and happy. We benefit personally and corporately in untold ways from Mary's interventions."[37]
—Phoebe Griswold

ARY SOMETIMES SEEMS LIKE THE attic ghost that will not rest. Her image is seen by the faithful in grottos and cloud formations, on hillsides, windows, walls, and highway overpasses. She "appears," much like an angel appears in Holy Scripture: suddenly. The faithful interpret these visitations as if Mary has some urgent messages for humanity, and usually that message is for increased faithfulness to her son.

Surprisingly, the quote that begins this chapter is not taken from a Roman Catholic, but from an Episcopalian who is, in fact, the spouse of the Presiding Bishop of the Episcopal Church in the United States. It is not only Catholics who look for these visitations of the Virgin Mary. However, some people have strong reactions against them, as well.

The Second Vatican Council, convened in the 1960s by Pope John XXIII, upheld the notion that Mary is the mother of all Christians. In fact—even though the Council is often criticized for having minimized the role of Mary to satisfy Protestant objections, it goes out of its way, in this passage, to describe Mary's "saving office."

> The motherhood of Mary in the order of grace continues [today] uninterruptedly from the consent that she loyally gave at the Annunciation and which she sustained without wavering beneath the cross, until the eternal fulfillment of all the elect. Taken up to heaven, she did not lay aside this saving office, but by her manifold intercession continues to bring us the gifts of eternal salvation.[38]

It is no wonder, then, that Mary is always reaching out to communicate to people. Forget about any boundary between the living and the dead; as we have seen earlier in this book, the veil is very thin between saints who are dead and those still living. Rowan Williams, the archbishop of Canterbury, recently wrote: "What we call holy in the world—a person, a place, a set of words or pictures—is so because it is a transitional place, a borderland, where the completely foreign is brought together with the familiar. Here is somewhere that looks as if it belongs within the world we are at home in, but in fact it leads directly into strangeness."[39]

Appearing Now in a Field Near You

That's the framework for understanding Mary's apparitions and visitations. Again, to quote that document from the Second Vatican Council: "The Blessed Virgin is invoked in the Church under the titles of Advocate, Helper, Benefactress, and Mediatrix." Her role and her names are similar to that and those of the Holy Spirit. In fact, in many ways, Mary is for the devout Catholic what the Holy Spirit is for the devout Protestant. The difference is that no one ever claimed to see the Holy Spirit standing in front of them.

There are shrines all over the world dedicated to the saints, to Christ, and to Mary, the queen of all saints. But Mary far outnumbers the others. Approximately sixty-five percent of all Christian shrines throughout the world are dedicated to the Virgin.[40] These places are both strange and familiar—particularly to the person who is coming to see the Virgin in a meaningful way for the first time.

Some of Mary's shrines have been erected in the most unusual times and places. Millions of people, for instance, believe that Mary has been giving visions and personal messages to people at Medjugorje in what is now Bosnia-Hercegovina for the last twenty-five years. The remote village of Medjugorje was not even on most maps of the region before Mary began to appear there in 1981. Today, it is a center of Marian activity; what was once a village of a few small houses is now a bustling center of religion and commerce.

However, many sites such as Medjugorje, and the messages from Mary that are heard there, are not officially blessed by the Vatican. Even though Pope John Paul II himself was reportedly close to calling Medjugorje a genuine apparition site prior to his death, it is uncertain, now, whether or not this will ever happen. In fact, only ten apparition sites have been officially sanctioned by the Vatican over the centuries, all but one of them in Europe, and all but one of those in Western Europe over a period of 103 years:

December 1531: Guadalupe, Mexico
November 1830: Paris, France
September 1846: La Salette, France
February–July 1858: Lourdes, France
January 1866: Philippsdorf, Czech Republic
January 1871: Pontmain, Brittany, France
July 1876: Pompeii, Italy
May–October 1917: Fatima, Portugal
November 1932–January 1933: Beauraing, Belgium
January–February 1933: Banneux, Belgium[41]

The responsibility for sanctioning new visions of Mary usually rests with local, Catholic authorities (rather than the Vatican), but history has shown that local dioceses are very reluctant to do so. Priests and bishops are often skeptics, just like most of us, and require tests for authenticity. Most often, they decide that the evidence is inconclusive. As a result, the experiences of those who hear Mary's words and see her standing before them are followed by a separation between private devotion and the ecclesiastical world of the church. In other words, the faithful still believe, worship, and pray, while the Church stands apart, often wishing that those visiting the shrine would be in church at Mass, instead.

Apparitions are treated with uncertainty throughout the Catholic world. For example, ten years after the much-publicized visitations of Mary to an elderly woman in Conyers, Georgia, I spoke with two different Cistercian monks about what happened in those days. One of them—an idealist and something of a saint—remarked matter-of-factly: "When the Holy Mother began showing herself down the road from the abbey, it was a tremendous financial boon for the community. The monks have been living off of that wind-fall ever since." The other, more of a realist, referred to that time as "A crazy period when an old woman claimed to see the Virgin in her backyard."

But still, people seem to see her everywhere. Clearwater, Florida, for instance, is another place that has received far less attention than Medjugorje. Since 1996, an image of the Virgin has drawn hundreds of thousands of pilgrims and curiosity seekers to the Gulf Coast town. It all began when Mary appeared to be superimposed on the surface of some windows on an office building. She stood there, in this image upon the glass, looking down at the world below. A shrine was erected at the foot of the building on Highway 19 and a crucifix was hung beneath the windows. The faithful kept vigil at that spot around the clock—until one day in 2003, Kyle Maskell, a troubled youth, hurled steel balls with a sling-shot through the top layer of windows, effectively decapitating the image of Mary. The boy was quickly con-victed of the crime and put into a foster home. He was then sentenced to ten days in jail and two years probation, and a judge ordered him to pay $2,300 for the damage and court costs. Today, Shepherds of Christ Ministries, who originally began leasing the building in 1998 in order to safeguard the windows, says that an image of Christ is again clearly visible in some of the remaining glass.[42]

In April 2005, a highway underpass in Chicago, Illinois, was the site of another image of the Virgin Mary. Just as Pope John Paul II was dying in Rome, a salt stain appeared on the Fullerton Avenue underpass of the Kennedy Expressway that very closely resembled the head of the Virgin of Guadalupe holding John Paul, supporting him in his frailty.

A spokesperson for the Archdiocese of Chicago, according to the Associated Press and CNN, said at the time: "These things don't happen every day. Sometimes people ask us to look into it. Most of the time they don't. [The meaning] depends on the individual who sees it. To them, it's real. To them, it reaffirms their faith." A large shrine soon gathered around the image, including an artist's rendering of the image in oils, as well as candles and flowers left by the hundreds, perhaps thousands, who prayed there. On April 25, 2005, according to the *Chicago Tribune*, even Chicago's Cardinal Francis George said of the shrine: "If it's helpful in reminding people of the Virgin Mary's care for us and love for us, that's wonderful."[43]

Similar to the Clearwater case, the Chicago underpass image of Mary was also eventually vandalized. Two and a half weeks after the comments of the cardinal were quoted in the local newspaper, a thirty-seven-year-old homeless man, Victor Gonzalez, was arrested and charged with a misdemeanor for painting over the salt stain with black shoe polish. He wrote the words "Big Lie."[44] At first, city workers simply painted over the image in order to remove the offending graffiti, but by the next day, a number of the faithful had carefully removed the city's brown paint, as well as the black graffiti underneath it, leaving only the original salt stain looking largely as it had appeared before the criminal incident.

Many other communities in the United States have experienced visitations in recent years, including greater Cincinnati, Ohio, and Tickfaw, Louisiana (fifty miles north of New Orleans). There is a rich culture and history of devotion to the Virgin Mary in America, but it is a snapshot compared to the feature film around the world. In fact, Americans owe the beginnings of Marian devotion in this country largely to the French, who occupied much of the northeast corridor of what is now the United States from the middle 1600s to the time of the Revolutionary War.

Appearing Now in a Field Near You

The city of Pittsburgh was the site of one of the first churches named for Mary. It is at the strategic confluence of the Monongahela and the Allegheny rivers, where they form the Ohio. Major and then General George Washington recognized the importance of this place for future shipping commerce and travel from the northeast to the middle west of the country. He knew from his Indian guides that it was called "the forks," and the British and the French had argued and fought over who owned this part of the territory long before the colonists decided to try and oust the King from their country. But it was the French Catholics, coming down from Montreal, who first lived among the Shawnees and other tribes and established the first place of public worship in the area, within their Fort Duquesne. They named their chapel "The Assumption of the Blessed Virgin of the Beautiful River," because the Ohio River was known in those days as the "beautiful river." A chapel still stands there today, and it represents one of the first spots in America dedicated to Mary.

Why do these places and images of Mary draw people so poignantly? What is it about Mary that so compels us? Ever since the Middle Ages, special places related to Mary have easily become pilgrimage destinations. There is enormous desire to connect with this greatest of the saints, and to hear what she may have to say from heaven, to earth. Her messages almost always touch on the same themes: Be faithful to my Son; pray the rosary; bring peace to the world, and do acts of charity. We don't need someone to come back from the dead, as Jesus said, in order to tell us these things, but still, we prefer it.

Hearing or seeing Mary at one of these special places is a very different experience today than it must have been a thousand years ago. For today's pilgrims, piety upon arrival at the special destination is the most common expression of

103

faith. There will be kneeling, prostrations, rosaries, candles, and all-night vigils, but we arrive in our tour buses and SUVs. During the Middle Ages, the journey itself was important. The devout would walk, rather than ride a horse or donkey, and penances and special prayers were offered along the way. Sometimes these journeys took weeks or even months; men often left behind jobs and responsibilities, uprooting themselves for the sake of making this heavenly connection, and women sometimes left behind husbands and children. Traveling to see the Virgin Mary was worth risking everything.

Some pilgrims showed too much piety, however. Margery Kempe, that remarkably "modern" spiritual autobiographer of the fifteenth century, recounts a time when she traveled with a group of pilgrims to the Holy Land. Before they ever reached Asia Minor, somewhere in The Netherlands, Margery was booted from the clan for her excessive piety: tears were flowing, fastings were turning gloomy, and she was quoting Scripture and praying aloud to the annoyance of everyone else.

The most troubling visitation of Mary—for Protestants, at least—occurred in 1830 in the Daughters of Charity convent in Paris, France. This particular claim only reinforces Protestant concerns about the easy use of pieties in place of deeper expressions of faith. A young nun named Catherine Labouré claimed that Mary appeared to her while she was praying in the abbey chapel. At that moment, Mary was standing (she is always standing, for some reason) on a globe of planet Earth and there was a green snake—symbolic of the serpent from the Garden of Eden, whose head Mary's son crushed—at her feet. She had her hands open, palms facing up and out, and light was shining from them in rays of light. Inscribed in an oval around her were these words: "O Mary, conceived without sin, pray for us who have recourse to you." On the reverse side of this vision—because, for some reason, it was a revolving, four-dimensional vision—was a large letter "M" in the midst of twelve brilliant stars. Below the "M" were two stars; one was stuck through with a sword and the other wore a crown of thorns. Above the "M" was a cross symbol. According to Catherine Labouré, Mary asked her to have medals made for sale that would bear these striking images. The "Miraculous Medal" was thus born in 1832, and hundreds of millions of them have been manufactured, purchased, and used in prayer in the 175 years since then.

MARY IN THE MIDST OF CONFLICT

Most of the famous visitations of Mary around the world have been linked in some way with a need for political or social reform. Her messages to humanity are always of a spiritual sort, but the importance of her visits have often served other needs, as well. She appears in times and places of terrible uncertainty and conflict. The circumstances surrounding the experience of Mary's presence are not always idyllic. Taken in chronological order, it is possible to summarize the primary Marian apparitions in history this way: Rural England in the years just prior to the Norman Conquest (Walsingham, 1061); Mexico during the colonial invasions and occupations (Guadalupe, 1531); rural and impoverished Vietnam and France (La Vang, 1798, and Lourdes, 1858); southern Europe at the height of World War I, as news spread around the world of revolution in Russia (Fatima, 1917); Egypt in the aftermath of the devastating losses sustained during the Arab-Israeli War of 1967 (Zeitun, 1968); and in our own time, war-torn Bosnia-Hercegovina since the early 1980s (Medjugorje, beginning in 1981). Let us look at a few of these.

Strange Heaven

Our Lady of Guadalupe (1531)

Mary appeared to Juan Diego—a simple Indian who had converted from the practices of the ancient Aztec religion to Christianity—and told him that she was "the one who crushes the head of the stone serpent." This was another allusion to the fulfillment of that biblical prophecy of the son of Mary crushing the head of the serpent who had bruised the heel of Eve in the Garden. But the addition of the word "stone" is critical to the story, and to the indigenous importance of Guadalupe. The native Aztecs worshiped a stone serpent god, making sacrifices to it as part of their religious practice. Our Lady of Guadalupe was saying that she came to crush all of that.

The year of the Guadalupe apparition, 1531, was at the height of the Protestant Reformation and just before the influential Council of Trent, called in 1545 as the first step in the Catholic Counter-Reformation aimed at recovering power, and codifying doctrine, in the aftermath of the Protestant upheavals. Trent reaffirmed classic Catholic doctrine in the face of Protestant criticisms, and this is nowhere more evident than in session twenty-five, when the Council wrote about images of the saints:

> Images of Christ, the virgin mother of God and the other saints should be set up and kept, particularly in churches, and due honor and reverence is owed to them, not because some divinity or power is believed to lie in them as reason for the cult, or because anything is to be expected from them, or because confidence should be placed in images as was done by pagans of old; but because the honor showed to them is referred to the original which they represent: thus, through the images which we kiss and before which we uncover our

heads and go down on our knees, we give adoration to Christ and veneration to the saints, whose likeness they bear.

A Mexican painter, Miguel Sanchez, created what he called the "Image of the Virgin Mary, Mother of Guadalupe" in 1648, and it further galvanized intense devotion to the Virgin as the communicant of the powerful new faith (Catholicism) in the new frontier known as "New Spain," Mexico. Sanchez made great religious claims for his painting and for Our Lady of Guadalupe. He compared her to the Blessed Virgin as she had appeared to St. John the Evangelist, the author of the Book of Revelation, chapter twelve, and said that God guided his hand in miraculously making a copy of her likeness. Since then, the image of Our Lady of Guadalupe has compelled hundreds of millions of Mexicans and other people around the world to revere her.

Lourdes, France (1858)

Bernadette Soubirous, a simple girl from a poor family, saw "a lady, both young and beautiful" in a grotto near her family home on February 11, 1858. She was out gathering firewood in the woods for her mother's cooking, along with one of her sisters and a friend. The other two girls had quickly crossed a creek, shoes in hand, when Bernadette had to stop and remove stockings, as well. As Bernadette looked up, she was startled by a rushing sound "that resembled the roar of an approaching storm." Later that evening, she told her mother, "I feel the necessity of weeping." She could not sleep that first night, according to her testimony— which has been scrutinized by Church leaders since those first days—and despite her mother's urging her to do so, Bernadette said: "I could not convince myself I had been mistaken." That was the beginning of Our Lady of Lourdes.

She would visit Bernadette—who had become quickly famous in her village and throughout France—seventeen more times over the course of about 150 days, and then she was gone.

Monsignor Ronald A. Knox, popular preacher and Anglican-turned-Catholic convert, preached a now famous sermon in 1934 in which he outlined the similarities between Moses and Bernadette of Lourdes, the young peasant girl who saw the apparitions in Lourdes. They each stood by a rock and found water; they were each shepherds (in Bernadette's case, hardly so); and they were each sent to a people in bondage with words for setting them free. Knox preached:

> [Bernadette] turned back towards the rock, and a rose-bush that grew in front of it. And now she saw the rosebush flaming with something more bright, more pure, more beautiful than fire. She saw above it the figure of a Lady. . . . [I]t was only in later visits that she realized what a grace had been bestowed upon her; that she, too, was to lead a world out of its captivity. . . . Do not think me fanciful then if I suggest that we ought to see in Lourdes a sort of modern Sinai; and that we ought to treasure the words our Lady spoke in the grotto as we treasure the words God gave to Moses on the mount.

Jewish tradition often refers to the "ten words" of Moses for what Christians more commonly call the Ten Commandments. Knox uses this phrase to draw further comparisons. Just as God gave Moses ten words, so did God give Bernadette ten. Hardly original, numbers four and five were: "Pray for sinners," and "Penance." But, numbers eight and nine hint at the money-making possibilities that apparition sites can bring to an impoverished area such as Lourdes: "Tell the priests to build me a chapel," and "I want people to come here." These were supposed to have been the words of Mary to young Bernadette.

The tenth "word" of Mary to Bernadette has had enormous theological implications over the years. Christian skeptics everywhere, both Catholics and non-Catholics, have wondered whether or not the tenth revelation of Mary to Bernadette wasn't in fact a case of a teenager misapplying theological words that she had overheard. Bernadette reported that the Lady told her, "I am the Immaculate Conception." Mary's Immaculate Conception had become official dogma of the Catholic Church only four years before Bernadette was visited by Mary. (See chapter 11.) It declared that Mary was exempt from the "stain" of original sin, marking her as unique among all people past and present. When Bernadette reported Mary as saying, "I am the Immaculate Conception," it was taken by some as proof that the disputed dogma was true. However, simply the way in which it was said—in the first person, singular, present tense—raises more questions than it answers.

Fatima, Portugal (1917)

The appearance of Our Lady of Fatima coincided almost precisely with the upheavals of the Russian Revolution. The Bolsheviks were outspokenly atheist and sought to tear down the influence of the mighty Russian Orthodox Church. It was also at the height of the First World War. Our Lady of Fatima, therefore, identified herself to three peasant children as Our Lady of the Rosary and urged all Catholics to penance and prayer. It was believed that she also shared three secrets with the children (two of whom died only two years after the apparition). The first secret was that there would soon by an end to the War, but there would also be a Second World War. The second secret forecasted the world rise of Communism. Catholics were soon enjoined to pray for the conversion of communists around the world.

The third secret given by Mary to the illiterate children in Fatima was not revealed until many years later. Our Lady of Fatima became central to the life of Pope John Paul II, as he never hesitated to see miraculous connections between the Virgin and the destiny of his own life.[45] Primary among these connections was the time when a would-be assassin shot John Paul in St. Peter's Square on May 13, 1981. The attacker was a Turkish Muslim named Mehmet Ali Agca. The shooting took place on May 13, the day of the feast of Our Lady of Fatima. John Paul, who was seriously injured, later forgave Agca in person, meeting him in his prison cell, and explained that it was Mary herself, in honor of her appearances at Fatima, who changed the path of the bullet to narrowly save his life. The third secret was a foretelling that such a thing would happen.

Aside from whether or not you believe that God works in that way—altering the paths of bullets in midair, directing violent storms at one town and not at another, and so on—what mystics often fail to acknowledge is how these personal communications with God can adversely affect others around them. If God enters into everyday human affairs for me, why hasn't God done the same for you? One man's mystical connection to divine intention is another man's spiritual darkness.

Twelve years after he was almost killed by that bullet, the Pope was given the icon of the Madonna of Kazan (mentioned in the Introduction to this book) by a group of American Catholics who had purchased it in Russia during the darkest days of Communism in the Soviet Union. The Americans relocated the icon to a chapel in Fatima, but later gave it to John Paul in 1993. It became one of the Pope's most cherished possessions and hung above his desk for more than a decade. When John Paul II sent the famous icon home to the former Soviet Union in 2004, it was his symbol to the Orthodox Church and the Russian people that the conversion had been accomplished—Communism had been effectively defeated in Russia, in no small measure due to the rosaries said by millions of Catholics influenced by Our Lady of Fatima. This is perhaps an example of how we hear from Mary what we most feel we need to hear.[46]

These are all images of a Mary who has tremendous powers. She is even believed to shelter armies and guide them to victory. Pope John Paul II, for instance, believed that Mary had been responsible for the violent salvation of the Polish people on more than one occasion. These stories are central to Polish history and involve the Black Madonna of Czestochowa, seen in paintings and icons throughout the country. Back in the seventeenth century, she supposedly brought victory to the Poles over Scandinavian invaders, which won her the title of Queen of Poland. Two centuries later, the "Miracle of the Vistula" was so named for Mary's aiding of the Polish army in defeating the Russians near the ancient river. That was believed to have happened in 1920, the year of John Paul's birth.

Similarly, since the thirteenth century the city of Siena, Italy, has called itself "the city of the Virgin," due to her ability to bring the people of Siena salvation from their enemies. Readying for war against their regional enemy Florence, the people of Siena were led by their local governor, Buonaguidi Lucari, to "give" the city to Mary, asking her for help in battle. Barefoot and penitent, Buonaguidi and the local bishop led the people of the city to the cathedral. Before the high altar, the governor went to his knees and prayed aloud so that all could hear: "I most miserable and unfaithful of sinners give, donate and concede to you this city of Siena and all its contado, its [military] force and its district, and as a sign of this I place the keys of the city of Siena on this altar."[47] The following day, in the year 1260, Siena won an underdog victory against the Florentines, driving them back, and saving their sovereignty. The ceremony known as "the presenting of the keys" has been re-enacted each year, ever since.

MEDJUGORJE, BOSNIA-HERCEGOVINA (1981)

As we mentioned above, this small village in the war-ravaged Bosnian countryside has not yet had its apparitions approved by the Vatican. Nevertheless, thousands have come to Medjugorje each year since Mary first appeared there in 1981.

The Congregation for the Doctrine of the Faith, the Vatican committee that judges the authenticity of miracles, has always been opposed to sanctioning Medjugorje as genuine, and has refused to allow any official recognition of it as a place of pilgrimage relating to the Virgin. Most commentators have pointed to in-fighting—between members of the Franciscan order, who manage the site, and bishops and leaders in the local churches, who would prefer to exercise control over it—as the primary reason for Rome's reticence.

Just as the evidence of saintliness is often gathered and even generated long after the death of a would-be saint, so, too, in the case of the apparitions at Medjugorje, further evidence keeps coming. It is believed that Mary continues to give messages to the original six visionaries (known as Jakov, Ivan, Marija, Vicka, Ivanka, and Mirjana) even now, twenty-five years later. These daily messages are sometimes delivered to one of the visionaries as they are giving a talk to an audience about what is happening at Medjugorje. Wayne Weible, a Protestant journalist-skeptic-turned-Catholic-convert, explains: "Never in the recorded Marian history of the Church has such an event continued daily for such an extended time. It is as if the Blessed Virgin is standing before the throne of God, saying, 'Please, a little more time—it's working!'"[48]

Praying by Hand (the rosary)

> [Father] wanted to get rid of the statue, but
> Mother said, "if she goes, I go." I think the statue
> was the reason Mother became a Catholic, so she
> could kneel down before her and not feel like she
> was doing anything peculiar. We would find her in
> there talking to Our Lady like they were two
> neighbors having sweet iced tea.
> —Sue Monk Kidd,
> *The Secret Life of Bees*[49]

*A*ccording to legend, Mary gave the first rosary to
St. Dominic in 1214 and showed him how and
why to use it. Dominic was fasting and praying
alone in a cave near Toulouse, France, seeking God's guidance for his life. He was freshly back from his unsuccessful
campaign to convert a heretical group known as the
Cathars in southern France. The Cathars disbelieved in
Christ's humanity; like the Manicheans of St. Augustine's
day, they saw the world as strictly divided between spirit
and matter, corresponding to powers of good and evil,
locked in combat against each other. They could not see

how Christ could have been born of a woman or fully human. They believed that this confusion of matter with spirit would completely diminish Christ's divinity.

Mary's message to Dominic was simple: Theological argument and preaching will not convince the Cathars of their misbelieving. Dominic had founded the Order of Preachers only a few years before for this very purpose, but Mary aimed to arm him with a gentler means of persuasion: her rosary. "Preach my psalter," she told him. In her book on St. Dominic, French writer Augusta Drane offers this paraphrase of the Virgin's message to the young friar:

> Wonder not that until now you have obtained so little fruit by your labors; you have spent them on barren soil not yet watered with the dew of divine grace. When God willed to renew the face of the earth, He began by sending down on it the fertilizing rain of the Angelic Salutation. Therefore preach my Psalter of 150 Angelic Salutations and 15 Our Fathers and you will obtain an abundant harvest.[50]

It was in the century before the Reformation that this legend first arose. Scholars do not know exactly how or where it came from, but the best guess is that the Dominicans came up with it. Rosaries—or prayer beads— and the counting of prayers—reach back to ancient times. They also exist in many other world religions; Christianity did not invent the practice. Hindu holy men have been carrying and praying with beads for thousands of years. But, since the earliest days of Christianity, monks in the Syrian and Egyptian deserts were praying and chanting each of the 150 Psalms of David, and then eventually, and in certain places and times, replacing them with 150 repeated prayers of the "Our Father," known as the *Paternoster*. They would count these on strings of beads, or by tossing aside one pebble for each prayer. Prayer ropes are also common in the Christian Orthodox traditions of the East. Knots are tied for each prayer, or a set number of knots are followed just as others may follow the beads of a rosary. In monastic tradition, where speech is occasionally forbidden, the hand-sign that you are going off to pray is to "fumble with thy thumb upon the forefinger in the manner of parting beads."[51]

Sometime during the Middle Ages, the Angelic Salutation from the Gospel of Luke—"Hail Mary, full of grace . . ."—became its own prayer, offered occasionally with the "Our Father" and at other times directly to the Virgin. The Angelic Salutation came to be known as the *Ave Maria*, which is Latin for "Hail" (*Ave*) "Mary" (*Maria*). You will come across many references to people praying 150 *Aves*. 150 is always the ideal quantity of numbered prayers, modeled after the Psalms.

Which leads us to why Protestants are often critical of practices such as praying rosaries. We often assume that anything done by rote is not worthwhile, and is somehow cheaper than prayers offered spontaneously. It isn't true, but we live with centuries of accumulated Protestant feelings against what the Puritans used to call "Popery." Spontaneous prayer can become just as banal as recited prayer. What makes prayer efficacious is the spirit with which it is done. Prayer beads are indeed intended for the creation of a habit of prayer, guided by something tangible, which anchors the mind as well as the body. There are Protestant rosaries, and Anglican ones, too; but let us look carefully at the Marian content of the traditional, Catholic rosary.

Most of the prayers that make up what is called "saying the rosary" are essentially Marian. Many of them are *about* Mary, and the rest of them are about Mary's son. But most important, when we pray the rosary we are consciously entering into prayer *with* Mary.[52] According to Catholic tradition, we are praying as Mary would have us pray, remembering what Mary would have us remember, and with the slow repetition and thoughtfulness that is characteristic of the woman who pondered these things in her heart. So many of the other prayers for Mary's intercession are like begging for mercies, whether it is a desperate teenage girl pleading not to be pregnant, or an executive making a spiritual bargain not to be caught in wrongdoing. Praying the rosary is much different. The rosary is a meditative prayer. It doesn't seek answers or quick guidance. It is a way of listening for God in the heart, with Mary's sweetness, attentiveness, and intelligence. As Sue Monk Kidd says in the quote that opens this chapter, praying the rosary is a way of imitating and befriending Mary, on the path to knowing God better.

Praying the rosary also involves the lost art of veneration. It used to be that Christians knew how to *adore* God, in Christ, and to venerate the saints, but this is not as true, anymore. To venerate involves both reverence and love combined together; it is felt in the heart and seen in the eyes. It is cultivated in silence, serenity, and communion. Veneration is the key to understanding the "look" of Mary in many of the most famous paintings depicting her at prayer.

The construction of rosaries varies according to tradition. Anglican rosaries usually have thirty-three beads representing each of the thirty-three years of Christ's earthly life. Orthodox Christian monks still tie strings of 100 knots called *chotki* (Russian) or *komvoskoini* (Greek). The traditional Catholic rosary is composed of fifteen decades (i.e., ten beads), each decade consisting of the Our Father, ten Hail

Praying by Hand (the rosary)

Marys, and the Glory Be to the Father, and each being recited in honor of some mystery in the life of Our Lord and of his Blessed Mother. During each decade we should call to mind the mystery that it is intended to honor, and pray that we may learn to practice the virtue specially taught us by that mystery.

The way of using a rosary is quite simple. The string of beads is held loosely in the left hand, usually to allow the cross at the head of the bead string to dangle. The prayers are begun by grasping the cross in the right hand and praying with it. Most of the prayers used with a rosary are prescribed, short, repetitions; they vary from Catholic to Anglican and other traditions. Some traditions will have one pray with the cross: "In the name of the Father, Son, and Holy Spirit. Amen" as a way of beginning things. The traditional Roman Catholic rosary begins with the saying of the Apostle's Creed and making of the sign of the cross. Moving through the other beads—which are of varying sizes—the prayers include Hail Marys (said on the small, uniform beads), Our Fathers (said on the less frequent large beads), and Glory Be's ("Glory be to the Father, the Son, and the Holy Spirit. As it was in the beginning, is now, and ever shall be, world without end. Amen."), said at the end of each decade of small beads. Then, the "mysteries" are announced, meditated upon, followed by more Our Fathers, Hail Marys, and Glory Be's. Many Catholics will follow Pope John Paul II's recent advice to pray certain "mysteries" (see below) on certain days: *Joy* on Monday and Saturday; *Light* on Thursday; *Sorrow* on Tuesday and Friday; and *Glory* on Wednesday and Sunday. Two exceptions are made based on the season: Sundays during Christmas—*Joy*; and Sundays during Lent—*Sorrow*.

THE TWENTY MYSTERIES

There are twenty prayers celebrating twenty periods, or mysteries, in the life and ministry of Christ in the traditional Catholic rosary set. These groupings of mysteries center on four areas in the life of Christ: the "mysteries of joy," focusing of Christ's birth and childhood; the "mysteries of sorrow," looking at Christ's passion and death; the "mysteries of glory," focusing on the biggest events after the Crucifixion of Christ: Resurrection, Ascension, Pentecost, as well as two events that mark the afterlife of the Virgin Mary in the Catholic tradition,—the Assumption and Coronation; and, since 2002, when Pope John Paul II added the most recent five mysteries, the luminous mysteries, or mysteries of light, which illuminate Christ's ministry and miracles. This brings the total to twenty.

Focus on these Events	Intention in Prayer
Mysteries of Joy	
The Annunciation	Humility
The Visitation	Charity and Love
The Birth of Our Lord	God, Reaching Out to Us
The Presentation of Our Lord	Obedience
Finding Jesus in the Temple	Discovering God's Will
Mysteries of Sorrow	
Agony in the Garden	Devotion in Prayer
The Scourging at the Pillar	Patience
Crowning with Thorns	The Love of God
Jesus Carries His Own Cross	Care for the Suffering
The Crucifixion	Care for the Dying
Mysteries of Glory	
The Resurrection	New Life in Death
The Ascension	Gratitude for the Church

Praying by Hand (the rosary)

Pentecost	Spiritual Gifts
The Assumption of Our Lady	A Faithful Death
The Coronation of Our Lady	Rewards in Heaven

Mysteries of Light

The Baptism of Our Lord	Prophecy Revealed
The Wedding at Cana	Christ Can Do Anything
Jesus Preaches the Kingdom	Discipleship
The Transfiguration	The Glory of God and Heaven
The Last Supper	God Feeds Us with Holy Mysteries

Since the lives and ministries of Jesus and Mary are so intertwined, many of the twenty mysteries of the rosary are also about Mary. In fact, all five of the mysteries of joy relate directly to Mary and her involvement in the life of Christ. Each is supported by passages from the Gospel of Luke. *The Annunciation*: "Then Mary said, 'Here am I, the servant of the Lord; let it be with me according to your word.' Then the angel departed from her" (Luke 1:38). *The Visitation of Mary to Elizabeth*: "'And blessed is she who believed that there would be a fulfillment of what was spoken to her by the Lord'" (Luke 1:45). *The Birth of Our Lord*: "But the angel said to them, 'Do not be afraid; for see—I am bringing you good news of great joy for all the people: to you is born this day in the city of David a Savior, who is the Messiah, the Lord. This will be a sign for you: you will find a child wrapped in bands of cloth and lying in a manger'" (Luke 2:10–12). *The Presentation of Our Lord*: "'Master, now you are dismissing your servant in peace, according to your word,'" (Luke 2:29). And, *Finding Jesus in the Temple*: "He said to them, 'Why were you searching for me? Did you not know that I must be in my Father's house?' But they did not understand what he said to them" (Luke 2:49-50).

Strange Heaven

The Presentation of Our Lord would seem, to modern readers, to be primarily about Jesus, but it is not. In the Middle Ages, this mystery was commonly called *The Purification of the Blessed Virgin Mary*, and it focused on the faithfulness of Mary to the religious law of the Jewish people. According to the Book of Leviticus, chapter twelve, any woman who had given birth to a boy must, at the end of forty days, bring the child to the temple in faithfulness to God's commandments, and as a symbol of her cleansing from the birth before God. As the church fathers noted in their commentaries on this mystery, Mary was not obliged to be purified from her birth, in the ways of normal, Hebrew women. Strictly speaking, Mary was not made "impure" by a man in her pregnancy; but Mary showed humility and faithfulness anyway, and showed her son how to have the same.

In contrast, the five sorrowful mysteries have everything to do with Christ and the Passion, and very little to do with Mary except that, according to tradition, Mary was a poignant witness to these events firsthand. As popular culture has made clear from the Middle Ages to Mel Gibson, Mary is a prominent figure behind the scenes, expressing sorrow for her Son, throughout the events of the sorrowful mysteries: *The Agony in the Garden, The Scourging at the Pillar, The Crowning with Thorns, The Carrying of His Own Cross*, and *The Crucifixion*. Chapter six of this book, and the mystical commentaries of Catherine Anne Emmerich, made some of this clearer.

Mary doesn't just lurk around the edges of the next five, the glorious mysteries—she is central to two of them. *The Assumption of Our Lady* (see chapter 11), and *The Coronation of Our Lady* are at the heart of what usually divides Protestant and Catholic understandings of her. These are central places in the Catholic story of Mary that show Christ honoring her outside of the word of Scripture. It is this latter teaching that results in artistic representations of Mary seated next to her Son at the throne of glory. It is believed that Revelation 12:1 alludes to Mary in her capacity as Queen of Heaven: "A great portent appeared in heaven: a woman clothed with the sun, with the moon under her feet, and on her head a crown of twelve stars." Both of these points of tradition date back to late antiquity, but both were also reiterated as matters of faith by Pope Pius XII in the 1950s.

The third mystery in this third grouping—*Pentecost*—is also about Mary, even if less obviously so. As noted, the Gospel of Luke is the most important document we have for the life and ministry of the Virgin. Luke was also the author of the Acts of the Apostles, the New Testament book that follows the ·Gospels in describing the events of the early church, immediately after the Ascension of Christ. In the first chapter of Acts, Luke tells us of the Upper Room where the disciples were waiting. They were waiting for what the Resurrected Christ had promised them: "[Y]ou will be baptized with the Holy Spirit not many days from now," and Luke was careful to point out that "Mary the mother of Jesus" was among them. In the life of Jesus Christ, Mary is there at both the beginning and the end.

When Pope John Paul II offered the last group of five mysteries (*Light*), he introduced them by expressing his devotion to the Virgin Mother. He always spoke very reverently of the rosary, and urged all Catholics to pray it each day. But also, he spoke of his belief that Christians must enter fully into the mysteries of Christ.

The contemplation of Christ's face cannot stop at the image of the Crucified One. He is the Risen One! . . . [In] contemplating the Risen One, Christians redis-

123

cover the reasons for their own faith and relive the joy not only of those to whom Christ appeared . . . but also the joy of Mary, who must have had an equally intense experience of the new life of her glorified Son.

These last five mysteries bring the story of Christ into fuller perspective. They focus the tradition more firmly on Christ, and bring the rosary, and Mary, back into Christ-focus.

Mary is still present in this last grouping. She was the first person to know of her son's purpose on earth, and so understood *The Baptism of Our Lord* as the initial step in his ministry. Also, this memorable event brought together the two boys, now men, who were born only days apart and whose mothers (Mary and Elizabeth) were both cousins and good friends. Next, Mary was instrumental at the *Wedding at Cana*, her son's first miracle, and one that he performed at his mother's bidding. Also, when *Jesus Preaches the Kingdom*, we can see Mary perhaps at the front of the crowd. It is also speculated by some commentators that she was present at the *Transfiguration*, and although she was absent from the *Last Supper* according to the Gospel accounts, John's Gospel portrays Mary as the most faithful of the disciples during the events that soon followed.

9

"Hail Mary, Full of Grace"
(and other evolved spiritual practices)

I could tell she had repeated those opening lines a
thousand times, that she was saying them the
exact way she'd heard them coming from the lips
of some old woman, who'd heard them from the
lips of an even older one, the way they came out
like a song, with rhythms that rocked us to and
fro. . . .
—Sue Monk Kidd,
The Secret Life of Bees[53]

THE AVE MARIA

WHEN THE NOTRE DAME UNIVERSITY
football team began attempting last second,
desperation forward passes downfield, quick "Ave Marias"
were often said both in the huddle and in the stands. Slowly,
the play itself became synonymous with the "Hail Mary"—
a desperation appeal—but of course, it began as something
much more meaningful.

The *Ave Maria*, or Hail Mary, is comprised of the statements of the archangel Gabriel and Elizabeth, the mother of John the Baptist, to Mary as recorded in Luke 1:28 and Luke 1:42, respectively. The first sentence was Gabriel's, the second Elizabeth's (with the exception of the explanatory "Jesus," the name of the child in Mary's womb).

"Hail Mary" often sounds too formal to our ears today, but according to Christian tradition, when we say it or sing it, the prayer brings joy to Mary. The real meaning intended, according to Hebrew custom, is closer to "Hello, Mary," or "Shalom." Similarly, when Mary is called "blessed" by Elisabeth, we understand this also in the context of Judaism. Blessings are important in Jewish prayer, and when Mary is called blessed of God it is more of a statement about God's goodness than it is about Mary's.

This version of the prayer dates to the early Middle Ages and was prayed fervently by kings and popes, but also by the majority of illiterate laypeople, to whom the Psalms and other written prayers were inaccessible.

> Hail Mary, full of grace,
> the Lord is with you.
> Blessed are you among women,
> and blessed is the fruit of your womb, Jesus.

The final sentence of the *Ave Maria* was added centuries later, in confident reaction to the criticisms of the Protestant Reformation in Europe, and officially sanctioned by Pope Pius V in 1568.

> Holy Mary, Mother of God,
> pray for us sinners
> now and at the hour of our death.
> Amen.

"Hail Mary, Full of Grace"

The prayer continues to evolve today, as well. Christians in Africa and Asia often add slightly different twists to its language. Christians in the Third World pray it with more desperation and less hope than do Christians in the First World. In some of these places, the Hail Mary is often a statement of bond between earth and heaven, seeking the latter to greater infuse itself into the former. Megan McKenna, in her recent book on praying the rosary, quotes a Jesuit priest from South America who has written down from oral tradition a contemporary example of the application of Hail Mary. It begins: "Ave Maria, of the third world, full of grace, all you who know pain, know the anxieties and the subhuman condition of your people, the Lord is with you, with all who suffer, who hunger and thirst for justice. . . ." Similarly, this new adaptation offers: "Pray for us sinners, for it is our fault, in one way or another, by our egoism and envy, that you, joined with the rest of the women and the men of the poor, the third world, suffer misery, totalitarian governments, economic repression, wars and blood and hatred."[54] Amen indeed.

Let me offer another adaptation that may speak to both Catholics and non-Catholics:

Blessed Mary, woman of peace,
the Lord is with you.
Blessed are you among women,
and blessed are you among men;
blessed is the fruit of your womb, Jesus.
Mary, mother of our Lord, and
faithful disciple above all others,
pray for us sinners
now and at the hour of our death,
that we may, as you, discover our
true identity in Christ.
Amen.

Strange Heaven

THE MEMORARE

Tradition attributes this prayer to St. Bernard of Clairvaux. His devotion to the Virgin was well-known. As is usually the case with the titling of prayers, *Memorare* is simply the Latin for the first word.

> Remember, O most loving Virgin Mary,
> never did one seek your protection, implored your
> help, or sought your intercession,
> and was left forsaken.
> Filled therefore with confidence in your goodness,
> I fly to you,
> O Mother, Virgin of virgins.
> To come to you, before you I stand, a sorrowful sinner.
> O Mother of the Word of God, do not ignore my
> petition, but hear and answer me. Amen.

THE SALVE REGINA ("HOLY QUEEN")

Salve Regina also takes its name from the first words of the hymn in Latin. Throughout history, symbolism abounds to show Mary as the new Eve. She is the "Mother of Mercy," to whom we always have recourse for prayer and intercession to Christ.

The origins of this famous prayer and subsequent hymn are in the first Crusade. It was recited on the battlefield with plaintive tones and spirit. Then, a few centuries later, it became the favorite prayer for after compline (night prayers) during much of the year in the monasteries, as an entreaty to the Mother of God to watch over those who sang it into the night.

All of us, the prayer states clearly, are like lost children of Eve, in need of the sweetness of Mary and the gift of her womb, Jesus.

"Hail Mary, Full of Grace"

Hail, holy Queen, mother of Mercy!
Our life, our sweetness, and our hope!
To thee do we cry, poor banished
children of Eve, to thee do we send
up our sighs, mourning and weeping
in this valley of tears.
Turn, then, most gracious advocate,
thine eyes of mercy toward us; and
after this our exile show unto us the
blessed fruit of thy womb, Jesus;
O clement, O loving, O sweet Virgin Mary.
Pray for us, O holy Mother of God
that we may be made worthy of the
promises of Christ.

THE ANGELUS: THE PRAYER
OF THE ANNUNCIATION

The precise origins of the Angelus prayer are uncertain,
as are the origins of most pieties in our lives. These things
tend to evolve rather than begin. One tradition has it that it
originated in the early Franciscan movement in Pisa in
1263, one generation after the death of St. Francis. At that
time, Bonaventure was the head of the Franciscan order,
and he may have instructed his brothers to remember the
Virgin and the Annunciation each day at dusk as part of the
daily hour of compline. The friars would ring a bell at that
time, and upon hearing the ringing each person was to pray
in thanks to God for coming to earth as a human, born of
a woman. The first pope to recommend the prayer appears
to have been John XXII, in 1318, which means that it must
have been a common practice by that time.

In some places around the world, the Angelus is celebrated three times daily, in the morning, at noon, and in the

evening, often still at the ringing of a bell, which symbolizes the arrival of the angel to Mary, or, the continual arrival of God in our midst. The name, Angelus, comes from the first Latin word of the Annunciation story: "The angel of the Lord declared unto Mary, . . ." or, *Angelus Domini nuntiavit Mariae*. The Angelus is a celebration of the Incarnation and the Annunciation—the occasion when God (or Gabriel) first told us (or Mary) the Good News. It is a prayer that is intended to be recited in groups, with a leader and responses.

This marvelous medieval prayer is still enormously popular today. The responsive nature of the prayer is common. The traditional Angelus comes first, and is followed by related prayers that emphasize the theological point: The primary meaning of the Annunciation is that Christ came among us.

The Angel of the Lord declared unto Mary.

And she conceived of the Holy Spirit.
Hail, Mary, full of grace, the Lord is with you. Blessed are you among women, and blessed is the fruit of your womb, Jesus. Holy Mary, Mother of God, pray for us sinners now and at the hour of our death. Amen.

Behold the handmaid of the Lord;
Be it done unto me according to thy word.
Hail, Mary, full of grace, the Lord is with you. Blessed are you among women, and blessed is the fruit of your womb, Jesus.

And the Word was made Flesh,
And dwelt among us.

"Hail Mary, Full of Grace"

Hail, Mary, full of grace, the Lord is with you. Blessed are you among women, and blessed is the fruit of your womb, Jesus.
Pray for us, O holy Mother of God,
That we may be made worthy of the promises of Christ.

Let us pray.

Pour forth, we beseech thee, O Lord, Thy grace into our hearts, that we to whom the Incarnation of Christ Thy Son was made known by the message of an angel, may by His Passion and Cross be brought to the glory of His Resurrection. Through the same Christ our Lord. *Amen.*

May God's help be with us always, and may the souls of the faithful departed, through the mercy of God rest in peace. *Amen.*

The Angelus is a prayer that focuses us on humility, using Mary's humility as our guide. It is supposed to be prayed entirely on one's knees.

10

Thousands of Our Ladies (feasts and titles)

"*A*dvocate. Advocate and mistress of all the faithful. Advocate and peacemaker with God. Advocate and protectress of those who desire to arrive at great purity for receiving Holy Communion. Advocate and refuge of sinners. Advocate before the Father. Advocate for the miserable. Advocate in heaven. Advocate in the presence of our Judge. Advocate of all. Advocate of Eve and the whole human race. Advocate of penitents. Advocate of sinners. Advocate of the most hopeless cases. Advocate of the most wretched and abandoned sinners, if they but come unto thee. Advocate of the poor. Advocate of the unfortunate. Advocate of the universal Church. Advocate of the world. Advocate with our Lord. All-powerful advocate. An advocate who is able to save all. Dear advocate and mediatrix with Jesus Christ. Glorious advocate. Good advocate. Great advocate. Great intercessor for all Christians. Intercessor for the entire world. Intercessor of our race. Intercessor of the faithful. Mighty advocate. Most gracious advocate. Our own beloved advocate. Perpetual advocate with the Eternal Father. Powerful advocate at the Throne of the Most High. Suppliant for sinners. Sweet advocate. Tender advocate. Wise advocate."

These thirty-nine titles for Mary cover only the category of *Advocate*, as meticulously compiled by the late Florent E. Franke, MD. In addition to *Advocate*, he had twenty-two other categories for titles including *Mistress*, *Model*, *Mother*, and *Our Means to Heaven*. Each title within these categories is cross-referenced to its source in patristic, papal, and other literature of the Church. This remarkable listing was originally privately published under the title *Hail Mary! Six Thousand Titles and Praises of Our Lady*, and is now maintained on the website of the University of Dayton as a part of their Marian Library. (http://www.udayton.edu/mary/resources/titles/HailMary.html)

There are as many names for Mary as there are attributes one might apply to the most revered of saints. We looked in some detail at the many *metaphors* for Mary in the Bible in Part One, but *titles* are something else. Metaphors function like adjectives; we make comparisons when we use metaphors, and people have compared Mary to many things over the years. When we compare Mary to Eve, we are drawing conclusions about Mary's role in the world, about her purpose, about her life. We are describing her attributes. But Mary's titles are more than attributes; they are ways in which we address her with reverence. Imagine if you were to address your most-loved grandparent or some other elder in your life as "Blessed Father" or "Wise Mother," to show your respect for him or her. Such titles for family members are uncommon, but others are not. In most families, there is a "Nana," an "Opa," a "Papa" or "Baba." In the same way, Jesus called his Father

"Abba" and encouraged us to do the same. Praying to "Our Abba in heaven" can be a very different experience from praying to "Our Father in heaven." Titles are names that say something about how we feel, and using different titles for those we love, or in our spiritual relationship with a saint such as Mary, can open up new opportunities for understanding how we relate to each other.

St. Thérèse of Lisieux, who was effusive in her love for the Virgin and her titles, wrote a long poem entitled "Why I Love You, O Mary!" in which she explains that the answer to her question is that Mary is so many things. St. Thérèse begins the poem by saying, "Oh! I would like to sing, Mary, why I love you, / Why your sweet name thrills my heart." She sings to Mary as "Queen of Angels," "Eloquent Silence," "Beloved Mother," and "Refuge of Sinners," among many others.[55]

When the Reformation took hold throughout much of Europe, many devotions to the Virgin were either eliminated or changed in Protestant worship. Sometimes, practices such as saying rosaries were even outlawed. A more modest example can be found in the first edition of the *Book of Common Prayer* (1549), Thomas Cranmer's adaptation of the Roman breviary. In addition to removing most of the indulgence system that Luther and others had been protesting for a generation, Cranmer's new book for public and private worship insisted that the Bible readings be read aloud in English, not Latin, and an act of the British Parliament declared that the Eucharistic cup would no longer be denied to the laity. Also, the 1549 prayer book retained only two of the medieval feasts that commemorate the life and ministry of the Virgin Mary. Although the traditional names were retained for those two feasts about Mary, the collects themselves do not even mention her name.

Strange Heaven

The 1549 Book of Common Prayer commemorates *The Purification of Saint Mary the Virgin* (more commonly known today as *The Presentation of Our Lord*) on February 2, and the collect for the day is prayed like this: "Almighty and everlasting God, we humbly beseech thy Majesty, that as thy only begotten son was this day presented in the Temple in the substance of our flesh; so grant that we may be presented unto thee with pure and clear minds; By Jesus Christ our Lord." Also, March 25 is the day for remembering and honoring *The Annunciation of the Virgin Mary*. That collect is also prayed in words that remove Mary from the action altogether: "We beseech thee, Lord, pour thy grace into our hearts; that, as we have known Christ, thy son's incarnation, by the message of an Angel; so by his cross and passion, we may be brought unto the glory of his resurrection; Through the same Christ our Lord." Since Cranmer's day, Protestants of all backgrounds (Reformed, Lutheran, Anabaptist) have inherited traditions of unease with, or shame in, the beautiful titles held by the Virgin Mary throughout the Middle Ages.

Every month of our secular calendar has at least two or three days on which those devoted to an aspect of the Virgin Mary may celebrate her. The most important month of the year is May, known as the month of Mary because of its long association with the beginning of spring, and new birth. It is in May—also the first month of Pentecost, when the Church celebrates the birth of itself, after the Resurrection and the Ascension—that the cycle of celebrating Mary begins each year. As Gerard Manley Hopkins wrote in his poem "The May Magnificat":

> May is Mary's month, and I
> Muse at that and wonder why:
> Her feasts follow reason,
> Dated due to season—

Thousands of Our Ladies (feasts and titles)

Hopkins provides the answer: May is Spring, "Growth in every thing."

All things rising, all things sizing
Mary sees, sympathizing
With that world of good,
Nature's motherhood.

Their magnifying of each its kind
With delight calls to mind
How she did in her stored
Magnify the Lord.

This ecstasy all through mothering earth
Tells Mary her mirth till Christ's birth
To remember and exultation
In God who was her salvation.

Mother's Day is always celebrated on the second Sunday of May, in honor to the Mother of God.

What follows are the most popular feast days of Mary from around the world. Each of them honors a different aspect of Mary, including her honorary titles (highlighted below in italics), apparitions (in bold), and aspects of her character or events from her life (roman). The list is arranged according to the Church year, beginning in the season of Advent.

8 December	The Immaculate Conception
12 December	**Our Lady of Guadalupe (Mexico)**
1 January	*Mary, Mother of God* (also called The Solemnity of Mary)

23	January	The Espousal of the Virgin Mary to Joseph
2	February	The Presentation of Our Lord (medieval names: The Purification of Our Lady, or, The Purification of Saint Mary the Virgin)
11	February	**Our Lady of Lourdes (France)**
25	March	The Annunciation of Saint Gabriel (medieval name: The Annunciation of the Virgin Mary)
13	May	**Our Lady of Fatima (Portugal)**
24	May	*Mary, Help of All Christians*
31	May	*Mary, Mediator of Grace*
31	May	The Visitation of Mary to Elizabeth
27	June	*Our Mother of Perpetual Help* (older name: Our Lady of Perpetual Succor)
01	July	Humility of the Blessed Virgin
05	August	Our Lady of the Snows
15	August	The Assumption of Our Lady
21	August	**Our Lady of Knock (Ireland)**
22	August	The Immaculate Heart of Mary
22	August	*Mary, Queen of Heaven*
8	September	The Birth (or Nativity) of Mary
8	September	*Our Lady of Charity*
15	September	*Our Lady of Sorrows*
24	September	**Our Lady of Walsingham (England)**
7	October	*Our Lady of the Rosary*
21	November	Presentation of Mary in the Temple

Thousands of Our Ladies (feasts and titles)

METAPHORS IN BLOOM

She is the flower,
the violet,
the first rose
whose fragrance allures
and quenches all longing.
More lively than any
imaginable scent
is the fragrance
of the mother
of the Lord most high.
—Gautier de Coincy (d. 1236)

Many of the most charming titles for Mary have been captured in the naming of plants and flowers. It is said that the actual fragrance of roses accompanies answers to prayers when they are offered to her, and for centuries, Mary's presence has been felt as both fragrance and natural beauty in the outdoors. Hundreds, perhaps thousands, of flowers and plants are associated with Mary.

The common lily, for instance, is also known as the "Annunciation Lily," and is pictured in numerous paintings of the original event. Lilies symbolize the Virgin's purity. Bright, blue periwinkles symbolize how Mary lived fully in the grace of God, and blue is a liturgical color for Advent, the season of grace made possible through Mary celebrated in the Church each year. Roses symbolize Mary's role as prophet, as she foretold the glory of her Son, and also, as she herself is said to have been foretold in the Song of Songs, chapter two: "I am a rose of Sharon, a lily of the valleys."

Many of these Mary flowers have superstitious origins, or are deeply engrained in the legends of Mary and her influence in the world. Marigolds, for instance, were first named in the fourteenth century during one of the plague epidemics in England. They were planted in strategic places near a home or dwelling in order to shine Mary's power and keep a family from contamination. The herb rosemary is said to have first germinated on the Flight into Egypt, as Joseph, Mary, and the infant Jesus fled Herod's men who were slaughtering all infant boys. According to legend, it is where Mary once laid her cloak in the grass that rosemary later arose; and it is no small coincidence that it is rosemary that we often use to season dishes of lamb. Mary is the herb for her Son, the Passover Lamb.

Still other Mary flowers are tangential to the stories of her life, but they relate to her by implication. The strawberry, for instance, as it is unique as both flower and fruit, symbolizes Mary's simultaneous beauty (flower) and gift to the world (fruit—Christ). Also, the three-petaled clover and pansy both stand for the Trinity, revealed to humankind through Mary.

Many people today will cultivate what is known as a "Mary Garden" as a reverence to the Virgin and as a tangible way of understanding the meaning of her traditional titles and attributes. One of the earliest of these Mary gardens is to be found on Cape Cod, in the small village of Woods Hole, Massachusetts. The Mary Garden of Our Lady at St. Joseph's Church, first established in 1932, is designed in the shape of a cross. In addition to the usual flowers and herbs named for the Virgin, many Mary gardens will often deliberately include wildflowers, as well, or weeds that flower. The inspiration for this may have originated with St. Francis of Assisi, who instructed his brothers to walk around the Umbrian countryside so as not to disturb a

single wildflower, as each flower, no matter its origin or
worldly value, symbolized the Virgin.

11

The Gate of Heaven (difficult dogma)

[Mary is] the gate of heaven, because no one
may enter that blessed kingdom without first
passing through her.
—St. Bernard of Clairvaux

Hail Mary Immaculate! The incomparable,
the most beautiful, the most holy, the most dear
to God of all his creatures! O Mary, to me you
seem so beautiful that if I did not know that the
highest honours must be paid to God alone,
I would adore you.
—Angelo Giuseppe Roncalli, age 16 (later Pope John
XXIII), diary entry, December 8, 1898.[56]

There is an old hymn of the Church called *Ave
Maris Stella*; it dates back to the ninth century and
was first put to music in Germany in 1704. It is
sung on feast days related to the Virgin. The first and last
stanzas of this hymn summarize the role that Mary is
believed to play in the salvation of souls:

Strange Heaven

Praise to Mary, Heaven's Gate,
Guiding Star of Christians' way,
Mother of our Lord and King,
Light and hope to souls astray.

Praise the Father, praise the Son,
Praise the holy Paraclete;
Offer all through Mary's hands,
Let her make our prayers complete.

Peter Abelard (d. 1142), the greatest theologian of his day, was the first person to teach that Christian redemption began with the conception of Jesus in Mary's womb. He also concluded, summarizing what many before him had felt, that "Mary is our mediator to the Son, while the Son mediates to the Father." Throughout the Middle Ages, Mary was described as our "advocate" before Christ. The Greek word often used to describe this role is *Paracletos*, the same word used for the Paraclete, the Holy Spirit. According to scholars, *Paracletos* connotes both advocacy and consolation—Mary's two primary roles throughout the Middle Ages. John of Damascus, in his sermons on the Dormition, described how the first Christians gave Mary the name of *Paracletos*.

Bernard of Clairvaux, Abelard's contemporary, agreed that Mary is our advocate. In one of his Advent sermons, he prayed to her that she would reconcile, extol, and represent us to Christ. In the first quote that opens this chapter, Bernard summarizes the feelings of centuries of mystics and theologians before him and since.

The day after Pope John Paul II's peaceful death in April 2005, Cardinal Achille Silvestrini, one of his closest friends and aides, said: "[The Pope] was not at all holding onto life. He was ready to trust himself to God. This is a man who had particular confidence in the Virgin Mary and felt that she was ready to welcome him and introduce him to God. I'm convinced that he has already met her. It is impossible to think otherwise."[57] Other people close to John Paul reported that his last words were his Latin motto of devotion to Mary, *Totus tuus*, "Totally yours."

These are the issues that most divide Catholics and Protestants. This pope's last words are an excellent key to opening what is devotionally and theologically intended by the idea of Mary being the "gate to heaven." This role puts Mary on the edge of salvation itself, but clearly not at its center with Christ. Nevertheless, the Reformers thought it was far too close to the center, and too far from what the New Testament says. The first Lutheran *Heidelberg Catechism* states simply and emphatically, "[Christ] is our Mediator." Philip Melanchthon, Martin Luther's friend and theological successor, called Christ "the only high priest, advocate, and intercessor before God" in the *Augsburg Confession* of 1530. Many subtleties are contained in the notion of Mary as the gate of heaven, including the dogmas of the *Theotokos*, her Immaculate Conception, and her Assumption.

THEOTOKOS (DIVINE MOTHERHOOD)

When Mary is addressed as the *Theotokos*, the Mother of God, it means that she did more than simply give birth to Jesus. But, what exactly does it mean? We can best understand the issues by looking back at the contentious Church Council of Ephesus, held in AD 431, where a struggle for ecclesiastical power pitted two church leaders against each other over the issue of the motherly role of Mary.

The West was represented by Cyril of Alexandria, and he eventually won the argument, and excommunicated the most eloquent voice of the East, Nestorius, patriarch of

Constantinople. But, this wasn't a dispute of West vs. East. In fact, the tradition of Mary as the *Theotokos* had, until the time of the Council of Ephesus, been most eloquently upheld in the East, by theologians such as Gregory of Nazianzus preaching from the same pulpits in Constantinople later held by Nestorius. It was believed that denying Mary as the Mother of God would be a threat to Christ's divinity.

The Latin word, *Theotokos*, means simply giving birth (*tokos*) to God (*Theo*). In its place, Nestorius argued that there were two, similar titles that were instead appropriate for Mary:

- *Anthropotokos*: giving birth to man. Mary as the Mother of Jesus.
- *Christotokos*: giving birth to Christ. Mary as the Mother of Christ.

But, Nestorius argued, from what he called "the precepts of holy scripture and the traditions of the holy fathers" that it wouldn't be correct to give Mary the name

- *Theotokos*: The Mother of God

because God exists from all eternity. Nestorius wrote the following in his second letter to Cyril: "Holy scripture, wherever it recalls the Lord's saving, speaks of the birth and suffering not of the godhead but of the humanity of Christ, so that *the* holy virgin is more accurately termed mother of Christ than mother of God."

Like Martin Luther in the early sixteenth century, Nestorius was responding to what he saw as too much of a good idea. An eloquent preacher by the name of Proclus had given a sermon in Nestorius' own cathedral just a few years earlier and had claimed that Mary was the *only* bridge for humanity to find their way to God. Not just a good and efficacious bridge—one to whom we could earnestly pray for help and guidance—but the *only* bridge. In response, Nestorius had begun preaching and writing, explaining that Mary's roles should not be confused with those of her son. Within a couple of years, he was condemned by Cyril, bishop in the rival see of Alexandria, even though scholars agree that Cyril was outside of his authority in doing so. Cyril was simply the better politician.

Soon after the Council of Ephesus was over, Proclus was installed as the new patriarch of Constantinople, and the people of Ephesus marched in the streets, chanting "Praise be the *Theotokos!*" and "Long live Cyril!" They wanted to believe in the dynamic power of Mary above all others. They wanted to believe that Mary could do what the theologians claimed she could do. They wanted that certainty, that clear path to God.

The summary of the experts at the Council at Ephesus was against Nestorius. The council members called it a "sad condemnation" which they did "with many tears." Their judgment was that Nestorius had blasphemed Jesus Christ with his words denying the motherhood of God to Mary. They said: "Our Lord Jesus Christ, who has been blasphemed by Nestorius, has determined through this most holy synod that he should be stripped of his episcopal dignity and removed from the college of priests." The dogma of the *Theotokos* emphasized what Nestorius had denied: Mary is the mother of one, united person, who is Jesus Christ, both God and man. The council members agreed that these two natures of Christ cannot be separated, and as Bishop Kallistos Ware has recently pointed out, they were also emphasizing that Mary did not give birth to a new person. Jesus was both man and the pre-existent Logos:

"The Incarnation did not involve the coming into being of a new person. When a child is born from two human parents in the usual fashion, a new person begins to exist. But the person of the incarnate Christ is none other than the second person of the Holy Trinity."[58]

The spiritual and mystical applications of this dogma grew enormously over the years following the Council at Ephesus. Medieval theologians soared high in their praise for Mary and in their claims for what her motherhood meant. St. Anselm (d. 1109), for example, once wrote: "To Mary, God gave his only-begotten Son, whom he loved as himself. Through Mary, God made himself a Son, not different but the same, by nature Son of God and Son of Mary. The whole universe was created by God, and God was born of Mary. God created all things, and Mary gave birth to God. The God who made all things gave himself form through Mary, and thus he made his own creation. He who could create all things from nothing would not remake his ruined creation without Mary." Anselm's claims are full of rhetorical flourish, but nevertheless, they do make serious claims for the role of Mary in the history of salvation.

In Anselm's first sentence—"To Mary, God gave his only-begotten Son"—he is deliberately playing on the meaning of John 3:16, which reads, "For God so loved the world that he gave his only Son. . . ." In the next sentence, Anselm has God giving his Son to Mary alone, and then from Mary, to the world. Christ is both "Son of God" and "Son of Mary," as if Christ's human nature was best summarized in Mary. Next, Anselm writes that "God created all things, and Mary gave birth to God." Here we have the old chicken and the egg argument; which came first? According to Anselm, in some sort of spiritual sense, Mary comes first, as the one who birthed God and, in that sense, "created" the Creator. Similarly, Aelred of Rievaulx

The Gate of Heaven (difficult dogma)

(d. 1167), the Cistercian abbot and saint, surely went too far when he said that Mary is "our mother . . . the mother of our life, the mother of our incarnation"? Mary is not even the mother of Christ's incarnation, let alone ours. These analogies resemble ideas common in the mythology of Hindu gods in India—an endless cycle of divine activity, creating and destroying. Finally, Anselm extends the providence or foreknowledge of God to great lengths of devotion to Mary, as if God, too, reveres Mary. "He who could create all things from nothing would not remake his ruined creation without Mary."

But despite the excesses of belief and practice, the *Theotokos* is still important for our understanding of God and faith. It is true that, just as there is a fatherhood of God, God is also a mother. We may not receive from God our mother what some medieval mystics would have us gain from devotion to Mary's motherhood: We do not become holy, just, or righteous. We never do, this side of heaven. But, Mary in her motherhood is the foundation of our faith and the most important model of what the people of God are and should be. As the Second Vatican Council made clear to Catholics in the 1960s, Mary is not to be regarded as standing beside Christ as an equal mediator to God the Father, but she is still a motherly model for us in various ways. The following is an excerpt from the Vatican II document called *Lumen gentium*, paragraphs 60–65. It summarizes the contemporary Catholic position on the role of the *Theotokos* in the life of faith better than any other teaching.

> There is but one Mediator as we know from the words of the apostle, "for there is one God and one mediator of God and men, the man Christ Jesus, who gave himself a redemption for all." The maternal duty

of Mary toward men in no wise obscures or diminishes this unique mediation of Christ, but rather shows His power. For all the salvific influence of the Blessed Virgin on men originates, not from some inner necessity, but from the divine pleasure. It flows forth from the superabundance of the merits of Christ. . . . Predestined from eternity by that decree of divine providence which determined the incarnation of the Word to be the Mother of God, the Blessed Virgin was in this earth the virgin Mother of the Redeemer, and above all others and in a singular way the generous associate and humble handmaid of the Lord. . . . [S]he is our mother in the order of grace. . . .

By reason of the gift and role of divine maternity, by which she is united with her Son, the Redeemer, and with His singular graces and functions, the Blessed Virgin is also intimately united with the Church. As St. Ambrose taught, the Mother of God is a type of the Church in the order of faith, charity and perfect union with Christ. . . . The Church indeed, contemplating her hidden sanctity, imitating her charity and faithfully fulfilling the Father's will, by receiving the word of God in faith becomes herself a mother. By her preaching she brings forth to a new and immortal life the sons who are born to her in baptism, conceived of the Holy Spirit and born of God. She herself is a virgin, who keeps the faith given to her by her Spouse whole and entire. Imitating the mother of her Lord, and by the power of the Holy Spirit, she keeps with virginal purity an entire faith, a firm hope and a sincere charity.

But while in the most holy Virgin the Church has already reached that perfection whereby she is without spot or wrinkle, the followers of Christ still strive to increase in holiness by conquering sin. And so they turn their eyes to Mary who shines forth to the whole community of the elect as the model of virtues. . . . Seeking after the glory of Christ, the Church becomes more like her exalted Type, and continually progresses in faith, hope and charity, seeking and doing the will of God in all things.[59]

Most important, the *Theotokos* shows each of us the way to become mothers for God—both in us, and in the world. The Annunciation brought good news for all of us, not just for Mary, and similarly, the *Theotokos* is our mother, too.

THE IMMACULATE CONCEPTION (REMOVING THE TAINT OF SEX)

This popular dogma is ancient and modern at the same time. It has been hotly contested throughout the history of the Christian church, not just since the Reformation. Both Bernard of Clairvaux and Thomas Aquinas, the most influential churchman and theologian of the late Middle Ages, respectively, disagreed with it. So did Peter Lombard, whose book *The Sentences* was the most studied theology textbook in the first European universities. Many medieval commentaries were written to deny it, and many others were written in order to explain why great doctors of the Church would indeed deny it. One of these apologies was written in the centuries before the Reformation by a Franciscan friar with a special devotion to Mary and yet a reverence for those thinkers who denied her Immaculate Conception. He goes so far as to explain how Sts. Bonaventure, the former minister-general of the Franciscan order, and Bernard of Clairvaux must have learned the truth about Mary after death (since they denied it, beforehand!).

I say that the Virgin Mary was conceived without original sin, and this is confirmed by examples. Consider a miraculous example in the case of the lord Cardinal Bonaventure.

A certain friar of the Brothers Minor prayed devoutly every night in the choir. One night while in prayer he heard a buzzing, as if of a fly, and he marveled at what it might be. For many nights he heard this sound, always over the altar of the Virgin Mary. Finally, he cried out, "I urge thee by our Lord Jesus Christ, tell me who you are!" Then, he heard a voice back to him, "I am Bonaventure. It shall be well with me, who am of the number of those who will be saved, but nevertheless, seeing that I held that conclusion that the Blessed Virgin was conceived in original sin, I must endure this my purgatory and pain over the altar of the Blessed Virgin. After I have been purged, I will fly up to heaven."

My point has also been proved by an example of St. Bernard's case. It is related of him that after his death he appeared to a certain man with a stain, and told how he bore that blemish because he had believed in the conception of the Blessed Virgin in original sin.[60]

The development of the dogma began in the fourth century, when the theologian Gregory of Nyssa, a leader in the Eastern Church, taught that Mary gave birth to Jesus without pain. Gregory saw this as an essential part of the gospel message, as it would reverse the curse of Genesis 3: God's pronouncement to Adam and Eve, after they sinned in the Garden, that women would endure pain in childbirth and men would toil for their food. It was also at about this time that it became important to the leaders of the young Christian faith to teach that Mary never experienced sex; she was believed to have been a perpetual virgin. And the legend grew that Mary was a member of an ascetical group, perhaps as a nun in an abbey, rather than a young peasant girl emerging into womanhood.

The dogma of Mary's Immaculate Conception soon followed, but did not become an official teaching of the Church until 1854, when Pope Pius IX called it "the doctrine which declares that the most Blessed Virgin Mary, in the first instant of her conception . . . in view of the merits of Jesus Christ . . . was preserved exempt from all stain of original sin." There are very fine distinctions at work there. It is not that Mary was miraculously conceived, as was Christ, but that her soul was sanctified by God's grace from the moment she was born.

There are other interpretations of what it meant, as well. Some theologians argued that Mary was born without the taint of sin simply because her parents conceived her without passion or eros. St. Anselm, for example, wrote that Christ's atoning actions applied to Mary even before her birth. Gabriel Biel, a fifteenth-century theologian, then argued that Mary's soul was pre-existent, created before the Creation, and therefore untouched by the Fall. I prefer, instead, this contemporary explanation by Catholic theologian Leonardo Boff of Brazil: "To say that she is immaculate does not mean that she did not suffer, that she was never troubled, or that she had no need for faith and hope. She was a daughter of earth, albeit blessed by heaven. She had human passions. Everything authentically human was present in her."[61]

Strange Heaven

THE ASSUMPTION OF OUR LADY
(RECONCILING SPIRIT AND MATTER)

The Assumption is the dogma about Mary most often confused with dogma about Christ. It has nothing to do with what happened to Christ after the Resurrection—that's the Ascension—but it has always been intended to show the similarities between the life and death of the Savior and of Mary.

It may have not been formalized as dogma until 1950, but it was believed and taught for millennia before that time. The idea of the Assumption reaches back to the ancient, Christian church. In the medieval era, it was even believed that this verse from the Hebrew Song of Songs, chapter three (v. 6), foretold of Mary's ascent to heaven: "What is that coming up from the wilderness, like a column of smoke, perfumed with myrrh and frankincense, with all the fragrant powders of the merchant?"

In 1950, Pope Pius XII formally declared: "We pronounce, declare, and define it to be a divinely revealed dogma that the Immaculate Mother of God, the ever Virgin Mary, having completed the course of her earthly life, was assumed body and soul into heaven."

The Gate of Heaven (difficult dogma)

Pope John XXIII later wrote in his diary on the annual Feast of the Assumption:

> My immediate predecessor Pope Pius XII proclaimed this dogma of faith on 1 November, 1950. As Nuncio to France, I was one of the fortunate ones present at that ceremony in St. Peter's Square. I felt no anxiety about this doctrine, having always believed it; during my years in Eastern Europe my eyes were constantly drawn to images of the "falling asleep of the Blessed Virgin Mary," in churches of both the Greek and Slav rites.[62]

The Assumption states that Mary holds a special place in heaven, where her body and soul are believed to have been assumed after physical death but before any corruption of the body was permitted to happen. Pope John Paul II often quoted from a sermon preached by a sixth-century bishop, Theoteknos of Palestine, to argue this point: "Christ took his immaculate flesh from the immaculate flesh of Mary. And if he prepared a place in heaven for the Apostles, how much more then for his mother? If Enoch and Elijah were translated to heaven, how much more then should Mary, who like the moon in the midst of stars shines and excels among all prophets and apostles?"

The Assumption involves several closely linked events in the life and afterlife of the Virgin. According to the dogma, Mary died as any other person would die, although according to the oldest traditions, her death was called a dormition, or a "falling asleep," completely without pain, anxiety, or sorrow. The Feast of the Dormition was first celebrated in about AD 600 and is still celebrated today on August 15. Jacobus de Voragine's *The Golden Legend* describes the event this way: "Then Mary's soul went forth

155

from her body and flew to the arms of her Son, and was spared all bodily pain, just as it had been innocent of all corruption." Mary's death was not like that of all other human beings—ashes to ashes, dust to dust. The curse of bodily corruptibility was not meant to apply to her, or, at least, it would be reversed by her, just as the imprint of original sin was removed from her at birth, according to the earlier dogma of the Immaculate Conception. Immediately then, after Mary's death, her soul was returned to her—she was "re-animated," as they said—and only then was she taken to heaven.

The Dormition and Assumption of the Virgin, from a twelfth-century mosaic.

It was generally believed that Mary's Dormition occurred in the town of Ephesus, where she had gone to live with St. John, after the instructions of Christ to the two of them from the cross. The following fascinating instructions from the director of a medieval miracle play to his players paints the scene of how this may have happened. Plays such as these are a good example of how medieval Christians came to understand the traditions of faith—also through icons, sermons, statuary, incense, genuflections—as most of them could not read texts.

> We must have a palm sent from Paradise for Gabriel to bring to Mary. There must be a thunder-clap in Paradise, and then we need a white cloud to come fetch and ravish St. John preaching at Ephesus, and to bring him before the door of the Virgin Mary's abode. We must have another cloud to catch up all the Apostles from their various countries and bring them all before the aforesaid house. We must have a white robe for the Virgin to die in. We must have a little truckle-bed, and several torches of white wax which the virgins will hold at the Lady's death. Jesus Christ must come down from Paradise to the death of the Virgin, accompanied by a great multitude of angels, and take away her soul with Him. At the moment when He comes into the Virgin's chamber, we must make great fragrance of various perfumes. We must have the holy soul ready [probably meaning an infant child, representing the soul]. We must have a crown encircled with twelve stars to crown the aforesaid soul in Paradise.[63]

The notions of Mary's Dormition and Assumption allow the Virgin's complete life cycle to become a near match to that of her son. This is what Dante intended when he wrote in the last Canto of *The Divine Comedy* that Mary's face most closely resembled that of Christ—not just a physical resemblance but something much more. All that is really left to the Catholic imagination is to find a way that Mary may have possessed a divine nature that pre-existed her earthly body, and she would completely mirror Christ. As John of Damascus said almost fifteen hundred years ago: "Just as the holy and incorrupt body that had been born of her, the body that was united hypostatically to God the Word, rose from the tomb on the third day, so she too should be snatched from the grave and the Mother restored to her Son."[64]

Other details can be found in this medieval play that mirrored the Passion of Christ to the death of Mary. The director's instructions go on to include a description of the burial of Mary in a tomb, the efforts of Jewish leaders to prevent her safe burial (showing the anti-Semitism that was common throughout the Middle Ages), St. Michael the archangel presenting the soul of Mary to Christ, a great light at the open tomb astonishing the Apostles, and an empty tomb later observed.

The dogma of the Assumption seems, at times, both unnecessary and mysterious. Traditionally, the Catholic imagination has been open to both of these possibilities, and still believed. As St. Paul wrote in 1 Corinthians, chapter fifteen: "Listen, I will tell you a mystery! We will not all die, but we will all be changed, in a moment, in the twinkling of an eye, at the last trumpet. For the trumpet will sound, and the dead will be raised imperishable, and we will be changed." The Assumption is one more way that the Catholic imagination allows Mary to model the faith for us.

WITHERING PROTESTANT OBJECTIONS

Many Protestants are increasingly willing to accept Catholic teaching about Mary that had previously been considered too troublesome. Lutheran, Anglican, and Evangelical theologians, in particular, have been meeting in ecumenical dialogue with their Catholic counterparts over the last few decades, and issuing various publications that show how far they have come from the days of ignoring and dismissing each other. These efforts are admirable, but unfortunately, they rarely affect the people of the churches themselves. It takes a long time for changes in attitudes and openness to different beliefs to trickle down. In my own Anglican/Episcopal tradition, I have seen occasions when the Angelus prayer and a statue of Mary have been introduced into worship at Advent, or a suggestion is made from the pulpit that Mary was the first true disciple of Christ, but to the anxiety of the majority of a congregation. Similarly, in Walsingham, England, where thousands of Anglicans make pilgrimage to a shrine of Mary each year, just as many Anglicans stand along the sides of the road and jeer their co-religionists. The Protestant mindset often stumbles on Mary, believing her to be too much a part of our Catholic past.

Hesitant to accept mystery over "truth," nevertheless, many Protestants are coming to realize that questions of truth are less relevant in the lives of religious people than they used to be. Dogma can make sense to people simply because it is beautiful. Perhaps no dogma of Mary fits this category more than that of the Assumption. On the one hand, it is completely outside of the boundaries of the New Testament testimonies; on the other hand, it seems to match the spirit and beauty of the Mother of God.

Anglicans have recently taken a step in this direction. In 2005, for instance, Anglican/Episcopal theologians joined Catholic theologians in issuing a joint document of agreement on the dogmas of the Immaculate Conception and Assumption of Mary. It is known as the "Seattle

Statement," named for the city in which the theologians held their last meetings together and issued the resulting document. The group consisted of an international gathering of delegates from the Vatican's Pontifical Council for Promoting Christian Unity and the Anglican Consultative Council, and had been meeting off and on for the previous five years.

According to the Anglicans/Episcopalians, the Immaculate Conception and the Assumption are now deemed "consonant" with the spirit of biblical teachings. Previously, the Anglican argument against belief in these dogmas had been simply that they were extra-biblical and therefore not worthy of widespread belief. That's now beside the point, says Australian Anglican Archbishop Peter Carnley, who was the co-chair of the joint commission that produced the statement. Carnley explained from Seattle in May of 2005: "For Anglicans, that old complaint that these dogmas were not provable by scripture will disappear."

It is difficult to imagine how such a complaint will simply disappear, however. Agreements among theologians are one thing, but a change in inherited perspectives of the people in the pew is something harder won. Many of these contentious dogmas can be traced back to the first councils of the early Church, at Nicaea and Ephesus. Christians over the centuries have often looked for this ideal of a pre-Nicaean, undivided Church, but in vain. Mary is usually the primary obstacle. But perhaps the removing of "extra-biblical" from the criteria for doctrine, which would mean taking a step back from what the Reformation taught us—would lead us there.

The Gate of Heaven (difficult dogma)

CO-REDEEMER WITH CHRIST (THE CHICKEN BEFORE THE EGG)

I love only Jesus
I love only Mary.
Let no one speak to me any longer
Of any other love in life.
    Love.
Jesus is my love
Night and day.
    Love.
Mary is my love
Night and day
    GOD ALONE.
—St. Louis-Marie Grignion de Montfort (d. 1716)[65]

There is no Catholic dogma that actually teaches or names Mary as co-redeemer with Christ. But, as we see throughout history, there are plenty of examples of the faith that have claimed, or almost claimed, just that.

In the above quote, for instance, Louis de Montfort places Mary in a role that seems to parallel her son's role in redemption. This sort of language has always made Protestants uneasy. It doesn't matter that Montfort's motivation was good; he wrote such things about Mary because he was primarily devoted to Wisdom, or Christ. He believed that to know and love Wisdom was to know and love the true Christ, "Wisdom made flesh." And, he believed, Mary was the path to coming face to face with this Wisdom, this Christ. Montfort's excessive devotion to Mary is aimed, like a hunter looking through a viewfinder at his target, at getting to know Christ more fully. But, as has happened many times throughout history, the role of Mary became too much identified with the role of Christ, in his thought.

The powerful tradition of Mary as co-redeemer can easily be detected in the history of art, poetry, and the teachings of the mystics over the centuries. For example, in one non-canonical text, *The Gospel of the Birth of Mary*, there is a scene added to the biblical accounts of Mary and Joseph traveling to Bethlehem for the census of Caesar Augustus, before the birth of Jesus. Mary sees a vision of two people before them on the road, one crying and the other, rejoicing. She tells this to Joseph, who in turn tells the young girl not to speak foolishly. Here, we pick up the text:

> Then there appeared before them a beautiful boy, clothed in white raiment, who said to Joseph: "Why didst thou say that the words which Mary spoke about the two peoples were superfluous? For she saw the people of the Jews weeping, because they have departed from their God; and the people of the Gentiles rejoicing, because they have now been added and made near to the Lord, according to that which He promised to our fathers Abraham, Isaac, and Jacob: for the time is at hand when in the seed of Abraham all nations shall be blessed."

This fascinating scene is an example of how the medieval imagination understood the Annunciation to Mary. In effect, it extends the Annunciation beyond the brief initial encounter that it was. The Annunciation itself becomes the new covenant between God and humanity, after the old covenant between God and Israel.

There are even conservative Catholic movements, today, aimed at recognizing Mary as our co-redeemer and the chief mediator between God and humankind. A weekly news-magazine recently reported that "A conservative lay [Catholic] group, *Vox Populi Mariae Mediatric*, has collected

162

nearly seven million signatures on a petition asking that Catholic dogma proclaim Mary as *Mediatrix of All Graces*, or the sole dispenser of God's graces, as well as Christ's coredeemer. The late Pope John Paul II was inclined toward granting the Virgin those titles," the paper quotes one expert as saying, but was persuaded against it by his then dogma expert, Cardinal Joseph Ratzinger, now Pope Benedict XVI.[66]

While Mary's role as mother of God is usually understated in Protestant teaching, the same is often overstated in traditional Catholicism and Eastern Orthodoxy. This dichotomy is perhaps nowhere more clearly demonstrated than in a popular image of Our Lady that we have from the Christian East. It is called Our Lady of Perpetual Help and was not widely understood in the West until it was brought to Rome at about the time of the Reformation.

The icon is a Byzantine-style image that scholars believe to have been created in the fourteenth century in Greece. It imagines the Christ child sitting on his mother's lap. She is quietly comforting him and giving him strength (he looks as if he may have tried to leave her presence, but she has held him there) to face what is appearing above the two of them: two archangels showing a vision of the instruments— including a cross, nails, and a sword—of the Passion that is to come. The archangels are looking at the child and the child is looking back at them, with some apprehension. Mary, meanwhile, is gazing straight ahead, giving Jesus comfort and also communicating to the viewer of this icon that she is our source of perpetual help, as well.

Could it be that Mary gave courage and fortitude to the Christ child? The author of the New Testament letter to the Hebrews wrote that, "Although [Jesus] was a Son, he learned obedience through what he suffered." Did he develop these human capacities—to obey, to have courage—from his mother? We certainly don't have any evidence that he learned them from anyone else. There is no person with whom Jesus spent more time on earth than his mother.

MARY'S MILK OF GRACE

Medieval Christians believed that Mary gave many things to the Christ child, including her love and care which she imputed *to him*, so that he might have these things in ever greater quantities. The most important metaphor for this love and care became a physical one: the milk from Mary's breasts. Tradition has it that Mary physically passed from her body to Christ's not just any milk, but heavenly food. Mary's physical body, due to the doctrine of the Immaculate Conception, was considered to be the purest human body of anyone other than her son. And so, the milk that she gave him was more than any other mother's milk; it was the perfect food, compared to the manna that fed the Israelites in the wilderness.

However, Mary's milk was more than an ideal, perfect fluid. It was also believed during the Middle Ages that both milk and blood define and transmit the character of a person. (Just as semen was believed by some theologians to carry original sin.) Coming from the most perfect moral human being ever created, next to her son, Mary's moral and spiritual character flowed in her breast milk. With that heavenly liquid, she fed the Christ child. Images of Christ sucking at Mary's breast, or of Mary offering her breast to the child, and by extension, to the viewer of the painting or icon, filled the medieval imagination. Stories abound of saints being fed by drops of Mary's milk in visions and in front of statues and icons. According to legend, Mary gave St. Dominic milk from her breast to quench his physical and spiritual thirst, at the same time that she gave him the tradition of praying the rosary. Bernard of Clairvaux writes of being sprayed with Mary's breast milk. These images communicated that Mary was the wet nurse for all who seek spiritual and physical wholeness.

Breasts were believed to be the place in the body where the blood pumps rapidly through the heart, and so, there were also men involved in this symbolism. *The Golden Legend* recounts a conversation between the apostles Peter and John as to which one of them should hold the honored place in line for Mary's funeral (even though her body was "assumed" into heaven, some of her relics remained). Remembering the similar conversation that took place at The Last Supper, Peter says to John: "You should be the one. . . . You were worthy to lean on the Lord's bosom, and from there received a greater stream of wisdom and grace than the others." It was believed that John's character was infused by Christ, because he reclined on the Master's bosom.

The Virgin's milk was the stuff of grace. It was the physical "evidence" that allowed medieval Christians—and then much of Catholic tradition that followed in its wake—to hold up Mary as if she were our co-redeemer with Christ. Throughout the Middle Ages, her milk was compared in power to the blood—that other important bodily fluid—shed by her son. *The Odes of Solomon*, second-century songs from Syria, describe the divine milk as coming from God the Father ("He who was milked") and the Holy Spirit as "She who milked Him." Mary, then, took of the divine milk and conceived with it. She is on a par in this regard to Christ, who is also described as breast-feeding his children: "And I was carried like a child by its mother, and [Christ] gave me milk, the dew of the Lord."[67]

Mary's gift to Christ goes back in time farther than the offering of her breast milk to the child. According to tradition, it extends back to the womb itself and the blood of Mary that nourished the Christ child, there. Mary's perfect body meant that she had blood that was as ideal as possible, and so, her womb blood sustained the fetus of Jesus as his first heavenly nectar, even before he tasted her virginal milk. Both blood and milk transmitted from Mary to Jesus was bodily food, but also heavenly food. Mary fed Jesus with spiritual life, not just physical life. Milk and blood both were believed to demonstrate the power of Mary's role as mother, her ability to nurture God within her.

These powerful symbols also carried greater meanings. The blood of Mary's womb was compared to the redemptive blood of Jesus' death. She gave to him so that he might later give such a gift to us. Similarly, Mary became known as the *nutrix omnium*, or the "nurse of us all," as her breast milk became a symbol to anticipate the Eucharistic feast. Christ fed himself at her breast in order to prepare himself to feed us. These images held medieval Christians in their grips, and Mary's milk became one of the most sought-after saints' relics throughout Christendom. Unlike other saints who died and were buried, Mary was believed to have been assumed to heaven, so there are no fingers or femurs of the Virgin on display in the cathedrals of Europe; but there are many ornamental vials of her milk. Even England—not home to many of the world's Catholic shrines—boasts Our Lady of Walsingham where the pilgrim road has for centuries been called "The Milky Way." Medieval Christians knew no better science of what happens between a mother and a child, but also, it made for a great story.

Finally, there is one more tradition visible in Christian art from both the East and the West; it is called "The Double Intercession," and seems to function almost as a new trinity. In these visual images, God the Father stands in the middle, while Mary is to one side, showing her breast, and Christ is to the other side, exhibiting the wounds of his Crucifixion. This is Mary's milk and Christ's blood as two fluids intended for the salvation of humankind. As Mechthild of Magdeburg exclaims: "Ah! Lady! Thou must still nurture us . . . till the Last Day. Then shall thou see how God's children and thy children are weaned and grown up into everlasting life. Then shall we see and know in unspeakable joy the milk and even the self-same breast which Jesus oft as infant kissed."[68]

But it is perhaps Bernard of Clairvaux who best summarizes what is meant by Mary's milk of grace, in one of his many sermons on the Song of Songs. Bernard extends the milk of motherly breasts first to Christ, and then to us. He begins by saying to his listeners: "Many of you . . . are accustomed to complain to me in our private conversations about a . . . languor and dryness of soul . . . devoid too, entirely or for the most part, of the sweetness of the spirit." Then, Bernard explains what is possible with Christ, through both spiritual discipline and God's grace, using images that are startling to the modern eye and ear:

> But if we persevere, there comes an unexpected infusion of grace, our breast expands as it were, and our interior is filled with an overflowing love; and if somebody should press upon it then, this milk of sweet fecundity would gush forth in streaming richness.[69]

The milk of grace metaphor becomes, then, something that can happen in all of us. However, any notions of Mary as co-redeemer will always stand in the way of an ecumenical understanding of the role of the Virgin Mary in our faith.

12

Unfortunate Teachings of Bernard of Clairvaux and Others

Jesus said, "Do not think that I have come to bring peace to the earth; I have not come to bring peace, but a sword. For I have come to set a man against his father, and a daughter against her mother, and a daughter-in-law against her mother-in-law; and one's foes will be those of his own household."
—Matthew 10:34–36

MEDIEVALIST G. G. COULTON ONCE WROTE, "It is difficult to see how the ordinary medieval worshipper can have avoided the conclusion that, for practical purposes, Mary mattered more to him than Christ."[70] Any reader of Geoffrey Chaucer's *The Canterbury Tales* will sense this, as the prologue to the Second Nun's Tale ("An Invocation to Mary") is full of references to Mary as the gentle mediator, the graceful, generous, and compassionate advocate for us in heaven. She is also seen as the prime agent of salvation for humankind.

169

Thou well of mercy, cure to sinful souls,
In whom God chose his dwelling,
Thou humble one, high over every creature,
Thou gave such nobility to human nature
That God did not disdain to clothe with wind
His Son in blood and flesh of humankind.

Now help me, thou fair and meek and blessed maid,
Me, a banished wretch, in wilderness of gall;
Think how the Canaanite woman said
That even dogs may eat of the crumbs that fall
From the master's table;
Though I, now, an unworthy son of Eve,
Am sinful, yet accept me, for I believe.

Dante, the other great poet of the era, offers a similar picture of Mary's role in the universe of Earth, Hell, and Purgatory. In Dorothy L. Sayer's translation, Dante writes in his *Purgatorio*:

Then of a sudden I was caught and drowned!
　　Deep in a trance of ecstacy; and lo!
　　A temple there, with people thronging round;

And through the gates I saw a Lady go,
　　Saying, with a mother's tender gesture, "Why,
　　My dearest Son, hast thou dealt with us so?

Nay—for behold now how thy father and I
　　Have sought thee sorrowing."
　　—(XV, 85–92)

There are many other popular texts from the later Middle Ages that offer prayers to Mary, giving her powers

170

that should properly only belong to Christ. For instance, this prayer has appeared in many prayer books over the centuries; it was originally written by an anonymous fifteenth-century Welsh-English poet and makes reference, among other things, to the tradition of calling out to Mary in moments of impending doom.

> We pray to life's source, Mary,
> Lady goldsmith of true health.
> She is rightly named the queen,
> Through her grace, heaven listens.
> To hell her power reaches,
> Above and across the world.
> Right, fearing pain, fearing wreck
> In the Channel, to name her.
> Right for Mary, whom I name,
> To be named a light-bearer.[71]

The great Cistercian abbot and the most influential of late medieval Christians, Bernard of Clairvaux, wrote lovingly again and again of Mary. He regards her as our prime example of Christian faith and our forerunner in heaven. He sings Mary's praises gloriously, comparing her to a bright star that illuminates the universe. He talks of how all Christians should mourn her absence on earth, now that she has gone to heaven, but that we should also cry out to her: "Draw us after you and we shall run in the fragrance of your perfumes!" None of this became a problem for the Protestant reformers. The trouble with Bernard's devotional teaching on Mary arose when he also explained, again and again, that Mary was "mother of our judge and mother of mercy." He taught that "She will humbly and effectively handle the affairs of our salvation." Martin Luther held Bernard in high regard as a theologian and spiritual writer, but eventually took issue with Bernard's teaching that "Christ is a fearsome Judge, but Mary is our comforter."

Bernard was not alone in emphasizing the grace of Mary and the fearsome judgment of Christ. Legends such as these abounded during the Middle Ages. (See the fifth legend in Appendix C for an example.) In contrast to Mary as the graceful source of life, medieval Christians understood Christ primarily through those occasionally frightening stories that litter the four Gospels. The Christ of the Gospels is not only summarized by the parable of the good shepherd (John 10:11–18), when Jesus says of himself:

> I am the good shepherd. The good shepherd lays down his life for the sheep. The hired hand, who is not the shepherd and does not own the sheep, sees the wolf coming and leaves the sheep and runs away— and the wolf snatches them and scatters them. The hired hand runs away because a hired hand does not care for the sheep. I am the good shepherd. I know my own and my own know me, just as the Father knows me and I know the Father. And I lay down my life for the sheep. I have other sheep that do not belong to this fold. I must bring them also, and they will listen to my voice. So there will be one flock, one shepherd. For this reason the Father loves me, because I lay down my life in order to take it up again. No one takes it from me, but I lay it down of my own accord. I have power to lay it down, and I have power to take it up again. I have received this command from my Father.

Another aspect of knowing what the kingdom of heaven is all about, according to the parables of Jesus, comes in the story of the king who put on a wedding feast for his son (Matthew 22:1–14). The king bade his servants to bring

172

together the invited guests after sumptuous preparations were completed. When the invited guests did not appear, the king asked his servants to go to the crossroads and to invite everyone to come, for the feast was ready. And the hall was eventually filled with guests. Then, Jesus says, "[W]hen the king came in to see the guests, he noticed a man there who was not wearing a wedding garment, and he said to him, 'Friend, how did you get in here without a wedding robe?' And he was speechless. Then the king said to the attendants, 'Bind his hand and foot and throw him into the outer darkness, where there will be weeping and grinding of teeth.' For many are called, but few are chosen."

Thus, the medieval understanding of Christ held both of these passages from the Gospels in hand. Christ was both of these—loving shepherd and fearful judge. A natural conclusion would have been uncertainty in terms of what to expect from Christ, while Mary, Christ's mother, represented only love and care, as any good mother would. There are many images of Mary's love and care, over against the terrible power of Christ, throughout the history of art. One medieval legend even has Mary sweating, begging, at the feet of Christ on the Judgment Day in heaven.[72] At other

173

times, she is imagined like the mother hen who gathers up her children in the safety of her flowing garments. The devout have often heard reassurances from Mary that she will wrap them up in her cloak, which is wondrously wide for all who are in need.

In contrast, the portrait of Christ can sometimes appear only fearsome. In the tenth book of John Milton's *Paradise Lost*, for instance, when God the Father is pronouncing to Adam and Eve, the angelic host, the other two members of the Trinity, and all of Creation what must happen as a result of Adam's and Eve's sin in the Garden, there is no mention of the *love* of Christ, or of Jesus the Good Shepherd. This narrative, told of humankind and the coming of the Son of God, is filled with anger and judgment, and only the slightest hint of mercy:

> What rests, but that the mortal sentence pass
> On his transgression. . . .
> Justice shall not return, as bounty, scorned.
> But whom send I to judge them? Whom but thee,
> Vicegerent Son? To thee I have transferred
> All judgment, whether in Heaven, or Earth, or Hell.
> Easy it may be seen that I intend
> Mercy colleague with justice, sending thee,
> Man's friend, his Mediator, his designed
> Both ransom and Redeemer voluntary,
> And destined Man himself to judge Man fallen.

After God the Father makes the announcement, Christ steps forward and formally accepts the responsibility to judge the earth. Then, in some of the most beautiful imagery in the epic poem—mixing earthly beauty with metaphysical events—Christ first descends to the earth below.

Unfortunate Teachings of Bernard of Clairvaux

Thus saying, from his radiant seat he rose
Of high collateral glory. Him Thrones and Powers,
Princedoms, and Dominations ministrant,
Accompanied to Heaven-gate, from whence
Eden and all the coast in prospect lay.
Down he descended straight; the speed of God's
Time counts not, though with swiftest minutes
winged.

Now was the Sun in western cadence low
From noon, and gentle airs due at their hour
To fan the Earth now waked, and usher in
The evening cool, when he, from wrath more cool,
Came, the mild judge and intercessor both,
To sentence Man.

The child born in a manger was someone to be afraid of, while the mother who bore him was seen as gracious and kind.

Bernard of Clairvaux was a man of his tradition, but he was not alone in his devotion to Mary before Christ. In the darkest nights of the Middle Ages—amid plague, Crusades, pogroms, death, and disease—it was common to see God's wrath more clearly than God's justice and love. Julian of Norwich, a fourteenth-century English mystic, believed similarly and taught that all true contemplation runs through Mary, and that Christ desires it to be so. Julian explained that Christ himself taught her to see Mary "in her bodily presence." According to this eleventh revelation (out of sixteen total) to Julian, we must be able to see Christ's love for, and joy in, his mother in order to fully see Christ. But, Julian continues: "I learned to long to see her bodily presence, and the virtues of her soul—truth, wisdom, charity—show me how to know myself and how to reverently fear God."

The word "joy" appears often when Christian mystics describe the Virgin. It is said that Christ looks on her with joy, and also that she looks on Christ, and us, even now, with joy. Julian of Norwich describes both of these aspects. She describes seeing a vision of Christ looking to his right side "with cheer and joy" at his mother, Mary, and then looking back at Julian to say, "Will you see her?" The implication is that all contemplative, thoughtful followers of Christ would literally *see* Mary and profoundly understand the meaning of her life, on the path to knowing Christ fully.

ENTER LUTHER, MONK AND REFORMER

There are actually times when Bernard of Clairvaux sounds like a reformer. In one of his many sermons, for instance, he contrasts the helpful "maternal instincts" of the Bridegroom of the Song of Songs, easily found in Christ and in Mary, with those in the Church "who have undertaken the direction of souls" and do that work through evil means. Bernard refers specifically to those in the Church for whom "the very price of the world's redemption is bundled into their purses." "There is no pretense about a true mother," in their greedy acts, Bernard exclaims.[73] He sounds like Martin Luther, who would denounce these sorts of practice two centuries later.

Luther's primary complaint with the late medieval church (of which he was a product) was its corruption through the practices of simony (purchasing ecclesiastical positions) and indulgences, where those in religious authority would promise heavenly favors to the laity in exchange for money. Simony and other abuses of religious power had already been attacked from within the Church, by Popes Leo IX and Gregory VII, but without enough success.

Unfortunate Teachings of Bernard of Clairvaux

Indulgences were an increasingly common abuse of power that was unchecked by Luther's time, and often used by the papacy itself to fill its coffers. The practice of indulgences infuriated Luther. After a short career as an Augustinian monk and professor, he became the most famous man in Germany over the space of four years through his writing and preaching against these abuses. He was a remarkably good communicator. "With the publication of the 95 theses in 1517 the unknown young professor of Wittenberg university became at one stroke a figure of national fame." Immediately after that, "Thirty editions of Luther's *Sermon on Indulgences* and twenty-one editions of his *Sermon on the Right Preparation of the Heart*— authorized and piratical—poured from the presses within two years (1518–20). More than 4,000 copies of his address *To the Christian Nobility* were sold within five days in 1520."[74]

But Luther was no enemy of the saints, and he was a true lover of Our Lady. In a sermon delivered in 1519, after his dramatic split with the Catholic Church had already begun in earnest, he criticized those who would use the saints to justify lewd behavior and taking money from the devout:

> We should look at the wicked works of [those who offer indulgences] . . . they organize a feast and a boozing; they have a mass or several held, and after that the whole day and night and the next day as well are given over to the devil for his own. . . . What do the names of our dear lady, Saint Anne, Saint Sebastian, or other saints' names have to do with your [work], which is nothing more than a gobbling of food, boozing, useless squandering of money, crying, yelling, sweating, dancing, and

wasting of time?. . . Why do you seek out the dear saints like this, misusing their names to such shame and dishonor?[75]

Luther also held the teachings of Bernard of Clairvaux in high esteem, but after his turn away from the Catholic Church, he exclaimed: "Bernard filled a whole sermon with praise of the Virgin Mary [and the Annunciation] and in so doing forgot to mention what happened [namely, the incarnation of the Christ]; so highly did he . . . esteem Mary."[76]

Quoting from Bernard's "Sermon on the Octave of the Assumption of the Blessed Virgin Mary," Luther wrote:

> St. Bernard, who was a pious man otherwise, also said: "Behold how Christ chides, censures, and condemns the Pharisees so harshly throughout the Gospel, whereas the Virgin Mary is always kind and gentle and never utters an unfriendly word." From this he inferred: "Christ is given to scolding and punishing, but Mary has nothing but sweetness and love." Therefore Christ was generally feared; we fled from Him and took refuge with the saints, calling upon Mary and others to deliver us from our distress. We regarded them all as holier than Christ. Christ was only the executioner, while the saints were our mediators.[77]

Mystics and teachers such as Bernard of Clairvaux and Julian of Norwich saw Mary's grace and forgiveness as clearly as they saw Christ's power and judgment. Perhaps most profoundly, Bernard expresses the difference between Mary and Christ when he wishes that Christ might be more like Mary in the days of judgment to come. He preached that the time of judgment should be tempered by feminine and maternal care: "[E]ven when he comes with power to judge, he should not appear to us in the form of God but in that form wherein he was born as a little child, and born of a woman, one of the weaker sex. Why is this? It is that on two grounds he should be implored to be merciful to the weak in the day of wrath and should remember on the day of judgment to put mercy before judgment."[78]

This is the sort of medieval understanding that was challenged by Luther and the Protestant Reformation. Despite Luther's own devotion to the Virgin, he felt it necessary to point to circumstances when even she can stand *in* the way, rather that *on* the way, to a true knowledge of Christ.

PART
THREE

Mary for All of Us

𝒯HE VIRGIN,
weighed with the Word of God,
comes down the road:
if only you'll shelter her.
—"A Christmas Refrain,"
by St. John of the Cross[79]

13

Martin Luther's Love for the Virgin

"Do not make of Mary a stone. For the higher people
are in the favor of God, the more tender are they."
—Martin Luther[80]

NEXT TO THE NAILING OF THE NINETY-FIVE Theses on the Wittenberg door, and the dramatic day when he made his famous "Here I stand" speech before the Pope, probably the next most famous scene from the life of Martin Luther was his superstitious prayer to the mother of the Virgin. It was during Luther's early adulthood, and has come to be known simply as "The Vow."

Roland H. Bainton, in his popular biography of the reformer, begins with this story, and nearly every biography, film, or discussion of how as a young man Luther came to enter religious life places this scene as the pivot.

Strange Heaven

On a sultry day in July of the year 1505 a lonely traveler was trudging over a parched road on the outskirts of the Saxon village of Stotternheim. He was a young man, short but sturdy, and wore the dress of a university student. As he approached the village, the sky became overcast. Suddenly there was a shower, then a crashing storm. A bolt of lightning rived the gloom and knocked the man to the ground. Struggling to rise, he cried in terror, "St. Anne help me! I will become a monk."

The man who thus called upon a saint was later to repudiate the cult of the saints. He who vowed to become a monk was later to renounce monasticism. A loyal son of the Catholic Church, he was later to shatter the structure of medieval Catholicism. A devoted servant of the pope, he was later to identify the popes with Antichrist. For this young man was Martin Luther.[81]

According to Catholic tradition and some of the non-canonical gospels, St. Anne was the mother of the Virgin Mary. (See the discussion of the *Gospel of Pseudo-Matthew*, above.) As Bainton describes, the young university student took his emergency vow seriously—an early sign of how he was to always take his words and those of others, seriously—and he soon left his studies behind and applied to become an Augustinian monk. The events of the decades that followed Luther's quick conversion are well known, and this is not the place to repeat them. However, it is important to see how his personal devotion to Mary was sustained despite his often bitter attacks on the practices of adoring the saints, and placing Mary in roles that properly belonged only to Christ.

184

Martin Luther's Love for the Virgin

Martin Luther was a lover of Mary. He often referred to her as the Mother of God (as did Zwingli, one of the more radical reformers), and he wrote a tract on the Magnificat, asking Mary herself for intercession to understand its depths. In it, he explained that "men have crowded all her glory into a single word, calling her *Theotokos*. No one can say anything greater of her or to her, though he had as many tongues as there are leaves on the trees, or grass in the fields, or stars in the sky, or sand by the sea."

TWO TEACHINGS OF LUTHER ON MARY

In 1521, early in his reforming career, Luther wrote his commentary on the Magnificat. It was composed during some of his most difficult days spent disputing points of doctrine before the Diet at Worms (a city in Saxony), and while he was exiled away in Wartburg Castle after his refusal to recant his positions. It is perhaps telling that Luther finished his written reflections on the Magnificat while he was in exile and very uncertain about his future. His followers did not know if he was alive or dead, and many of them feared the worst, comparing Luther's trial before the Diet at Worms to the trial of Christ before the high priests.

After a month spent working on the Magnificat in Wartburg, Luther finally sent the document along to the printer. Still in infancy, the printing process of the day could not keep up with demand, and Luther had two months of waiting, lonely and worried, before his commentary would return in printed form. Before the printed text arrived, Luther wrote to Philip Melanchthon, the heir apparent to what later became Lutheranism, saying, "I am amazed that my Magnificat is not finished yet. . . . Who knows whether this may not be the end of my ministry? . . . Yet I have not lived in vain."[82]

The majority of the treatise is fairly ordinary, differing little from previous exhortations to the faithful to know and understand Mary. Luther explains what it means when a soul magnifies the Lord, what it means for one's spirit to rejoice in God, our Savior, and so on, explicating the phrases from Mary's great song through frequent allusion to the Hebrew prophets, the psalms, and the teachings of the apostle Paul. His primary purpose appears to be instructive and explanatory.

But in addition, Luther clearly wants to distinguish Mary from the idolized version that he felt she had become in the medieval church. Mary is the Mother of God, but her blessedness is the result of God's grace alone. He writes: "Not her humility but God's regard is to be praised. When a prince takes a poor beggar by the hand, it is not the beggar's lowliness but the prince's grace and goodness that is to be commended."[83] Luther also sought to reinterpret centuries of interpretation of Mary's phrase, "All generations will call me blessed." He explains that the greatest work that God can ever do is to "regard us," as God regarded Mary.

> For where it comes to pass that God turns His face toward one to regard him, there is nothing but grace and salvation, and all gifts and works must follow. . . . Note that [Mary] does not say men will speak all manner of good of her, praise her virtues, exalt her virginity or her humility, or sing of what she has done. But for this one thing alone, that God regarded her, men will call her blessed. That is to give all the glory to God as completely as it can be done. . . . Not she is praised thereby, but God's grace toward her.[84]

Martin Luther's Love for the Virgin

Luther disputed the Catholic notion of Mary being specially chosen by God and therefore, without sin or somehow with her sins cleaned away. He insisted on applying one of his foundational Protestant principles even to Mary's case: *sola fide*, "by faith alone." He wrote: "Through *sola fide* was she saved and freed from sin." He wanted to be sure that Protestants do not praise Mary herself, but rather, praise only what God has done in her by grace. But, just as instructive to Protestants then and now, Luther remained devoted to her as a spiritual model and guide throughout his life. Somewhat mysteriously and abruptly, he concludes his short treatise on the *Theotokos* by saying: "It needs to be pondered in the heart what it means to be the Mother of God,"[85] And he composed this simple prayer to Mary, which he believed was an appropriate way for Protestant Christians to pray to the Virgin Mother:

> O Blessed Virgin,
> Mother of God,
> You were nothing and all despised;
> yet God in His grace regarded you and
> worked such great things in you.
> You were worthy of none of them,
> but the rich and abundant grace of God
> was upon you, far above any merit of yours.
> Hail to you!
> Blessed are you, now and forever,
> In finding such a God.[86]

Luther's second important teaching on Mary comes from a sermon preached on the celebration of the Nativity. In very practical language, the reformer portrays the scene of the Nativity: the dirtiness of the inn, the lack of help in delivering the baby, the cold manger without warm water to comfort and wash. "I am amazed that the little one did not freeze," he reflects. Then, Luther offers his meditation on the meaning of the Nativity as a glimpse into the graciousness of our Lord, offering a new vision to those who had begun to see Christ with eyes of fear and dread.

> Behold Christ lying in the lap of his young mother. What can be sweeter than the Babe, what more lovely than the mother! . . . Yet all that is belongs to him, that your conscience should not fear but take comfort in him. Doubt nothing. To me there is no greater consolation given to mankind than this, that Christ became man, a child, a babe, playing in the lap and at the breasts of his most gracious mother. Who is there whom this sight would not comfort? Now is overcome the power of sin, death, hell, conscience, and guilt, if you come to this gurgling Babe and believe that he is come, not to judge you, but to save.[87]

He turns the formula of Sts. Bernard and Julian (and many others) around. The babe in the manger is the image of a Savior, not a Judge.

In all of his preaching and writing about Mary, Luther continued to see her as a primary means by which sinners may come to God. She points the way to God. Luther summarizes his position by explaining that Mary would not wish to be exalted on her own merits: "What do you suppose would please her more than to have you come through her to God this way, and learn from her to put your hope and trust in Him, notwithstanding your despised and lowly estate, in life as well as in death? She does not want you to come to her, but through her to God."[88] At the same time, while Luther preached that the grace of God is freely given, he also could not help praising Mary's huge heart and ready acceptance of that grace, which was not at all ordinary:

> Oh, how simple and pure a heart was hers, how strange a soul was this! What great things are hidden here under this lowly exterior! How many came in contact with her, talked, and ate and drank with her, who perhaps despised her and counted her but a common, poor, and simple village maiden, and who, had they known, would have fled from her in terror.[89]

WHOM DOES GOD CHOOSE?

Perhaps this is the point on which Luther's reforms most benefited the Church, both then and now: He distinguishes between God's grace, freely given, and our good works, devoutly earned.

What are the qualities of those whom God chooses? What made God choose Mary? Was it an expression of God's grace, freely and lovingly given, or did Mary somehow deserve God's gift to her?

Centuries of Catholic tradition would have us understand that God chose Mary because of her holiness, purity, and grace. John Henry Newman once preached: "Who can estimate the holiness and perfection of her, who was chosen to be the Mother of Christ? If to him that hath, more is given, and holiness and Divine favor go together (and this we are expressly told), what must have been the transcendent purity of her, whom the Creator Spirit condescended to overshadow with His miraculous presence?" But is that really how God works?

In contrast, Soren Kierkegaard, a later Lutheran, explains that if you are considered righteous by others, and regularly invited to be in a position of leadership in your church, it isn't Jesus Christ that you are following. In contrast to centuries of teaching as to what the "personality" of sainthood might be, Kierkegaard says, "It appears that to be a Christian, to belong truly to Christ . . . in truth should mean in the world, in the eyes of men, to be abased, that it should mean all possible hardships, every possible sort of derision and insult, and mean at last to be punished as a criminal!"[90]

Perhaps it is this spirit—of understanding that followers of Christ do not usually conform to a particular look, or attitude, or personality—that is Luther's contribution to how Mary is a path to God today. She is many paths, not one, or even a few. She is our guide to Christ because of her multitudes, not just her simple *fiat*. Catholic nun and teacher Sr. Joan Chittister recently echoed this idea—which got her into trouble with many traditional Catholics—in a booklet titled *Mary, Wellspring of Peace: A Contemporary Novena:* "A close reading of scripture reveals a woman immersed in the same pressing issues that echo in our times. Mary was unwed and pregnant, an advocate for the oppressed, a political refugee, a single parent, a mother of a condemned prisoner, a Third World woman, a liberator, a widow, the first disciple." These are images of the Mary of Nazareth who speaks to our world today. She is a myriad of things, not simply the idealized Mary, Queen of Heaven. Mary stands for freedom and justice as much as for quiet faith. The Mary of history would be a spiritual model for us even if she wasn't sweet and attractive.

CHAPTER

14

The Feminine Face of God

Jesus Christ is not known as He ought to be
because Mary has been up to this time unknown.
—St. Louis-Marie Grignion de Montfort

INCE THE DAYS OF THE REFORMATION, AND
the devastating effect that it had on devotion to
Mary, Catholic critics have often complained
that Mary needs more attention. Frederick William Faber,
one of the most influential Catholic churchmen of Victorian
England, once explained:

> Devotion to [Mary] is low and thin and poor. It is
> frightened out of its wits by the sneers of heresy. It is
> always . . . wishing to make Mary so little of a Mary
> that Protestants may feel at ease about her. . . . It is not
> the prominent characteristic of our religion which it
> ought to be. It has no faith in itself.[91]

191

And so, traditions swelled to the point of making Mary nearly into a god. She is imagined to be sitting in heaven, cocking her ear to hear our distresses. One seventeenth-century hymn written by F.W. Weatherell and harmonized by J.S. Bach, paints this picture. It has been sung in churches for centuries.

> Mary immaculate, star of the morning,
> Chosen before the creation began,
> Chosen to bring, for thy bridal adorning,
> Woe to the serpent and rescue to man.

> Here, in an orbit of shadow and sadness,
> Veiling thy splendor, thy course thou hast run;
> Now thou art throned in all glory and gladness,
> Crowned by the hand of the savior and Son.

> Sinners, we worship thy sinless perfection;
> Fallen and weak, for thy pity we plead;
> Grant us the shield of thy sovereign protection,
> Measure thine aid by the depth of our need.

> Bend from thy throne at the voice of our crying,
> Bend to this earth which thy footsteps have trod;
> Stretch out thine arms to us, living and dying,
> Mary immaculate, Mother of God.

In recent centuries, these ideas have gained momentum. One of the most popular Catholic devotees of the Virgin in history, St. Louis de Montfort, fueled interest in Mary's feminine face of God in his book *True Devotion to Mary,* published in 1842. Montfort uses extravagant images and phrases to describe her role. He was effusive in his praise of

Mary as an archetype for our lives, as a mediator to her son, and as something close to a divine figure herself, as in this prayer.

> Hail Mary, beloved Daughter of the Eternal Father! Hail Mary, admirable Mother of the Son! Hail Mary, faithful spouse of the Holy Ghost! Hail Mary, my dear Mother, my loving Mistress, my powerful sovereign! Hail my joy, my glory, my heart and my soul! Thou art all mine by mercy, and I am all thine by justice. But I am not yet sufficiently thine. I now give myself wholly to thee without keeping anything back for myself or others. If thou still seest in me anything which does not belong to thee, I beseech thee to take it and to make thyself the absolute Mistress of all that is mine. Destroy in me all that may be displeasing to God, root it up and bring it to nought; place and cultivate in me everything that is pleasing to thee. Amen.

Ever since the days of the early Christian church, there have been people who have believed that Mary is the feminine face of God. She is not only greater than the prophets because she gave the only-begotten Son to the world. She was also wedded to God in order to produce the child,

Jesus, and was imagined by those same prophets when they spoke of the feminine side of God. When Mary stands for the Eternal or Divine Feminine we see the suffering mother (*Mater Dolorosa*) has become the glorious, heavenly mother (*Mater Gloriosa*).

These ideas have taken their inspiration, in part, from Jesus' teaching that we must have the faith of children in order to enter the kingdom of heaven. How can we learn to have the faith of children without a good mother? All children benefit from a good mother, and Mary can be our spiritual mother, an example and guide. Seen from another perspective, some both inside and outside of the churches today believe that we need a "feminine" perspective of faith. Just as we have been formed by God the Father, we would do well to learn from God as Mother, glimpsed in the person of the Virgin Mary.

Mary as the Divine Feminine relates back to the dogma of her Assumption. Not only did she not die (she fell asleep), but she was quickly assumed to heaven, and crowned by Christ who prepared the way. Many Christians believe that Jesus suggests these ideas in Luke's Gospel, chapter ten, when Jesus said to Martha, about Mary's lack of interest in worldly things: "Mary has chosen the better part, which will not be taken from her." (However, most scholars agree today that the Mary in this story is not the Virgin Mary.)

"TO JESUS THROUGH MARY"

Pope John XXIII once referred to this as "the familiar but precious phrase." Catholics have long believed that Mary is the most effective conduit to Jesus. The Annunciation first announced it, and her special role continues. The Mary who held the Christ child then later held her crucified son, witnessing the consummation of what was begun when the archangel Gabriel first came to her. In fact, John XXIII continues, expressing exactly why the Virgin is held dearly as a spiritual mother by millions of Catholics today: "[T]his life of mine, now nearing its sunset, could find no better end than in the concentration of all my thoughts in Jesus, the Son of Mary, who holds him out to me in her arms for the joy and comfort of my soul."[92]

Similarly, Louis de Montfort believed that, just as Mary mediated the birth of Christ into humanity, so too does she remain the chief mediator between sinners and Christ today. Mary shows all people the spiritual, mystical way to God through Christ. Just as God sought to incarnate himself in Mary, so today God wishes "to have children by Mary," and to "form Himself" in us every day through our devotion to her.[93]

Montfort explains the Immaculate Conception very clearly and lovingly—and with an emphasis on the intrinsic value of Mary—when he writes: "God the Son descended into her virginal womb, as the New Adam into His terrestrial paradise, to take His pleasure there, and to work in secret marvels of grace." Similarly, the thirty years of Christ's hidden life, before the public ministry of which the Gospels principally treat, take on great meaning for Montfort's devotion to Mary. Mary knows her son as no other person does, as, during those thirty years, Christ was "hiding His splendors from all creatures here below, and revealing them to Mary only."[94]

These images of Mary emphasize her value and place in history, as well as in eternity. Dante wrote beautifully at the end of *The Divine Comedy*, speaking the following words in the voice of Bernard of Clairvaux for all of those who would finally ascend the hill of the Lord:

Look now into the face that unto Christ
Hath most resemblance; for its brightness only
Is able to prepare thee to see Christ.
On her did I behold so great a gladness
Rain down, borne onward in the holy minds
Created through that altitude to fly,
That whatsoever I had seen before
Did not suspend me in such admiration,
Nor show me such similitude of God.
(Canto XXXII)

Mary leads the way.

But just as very few non-Catholics would agree that
Mary is all that these elaborate claims make out for her, she
is nevertheless much more than Protestants commonly
imagine. She is both a path to God, available to us, as well
as a symbol of wisdom in and of herself—a guide.
Protestants will often quibble with the simple notion of con-
sidering Mary alone—apart from her son, Jesus Christ. But
this doesn't need to threaten the theology of Protestantism;
it serves to remind the Protestant imagination that we must
be remade in the image of the motherhood of God, imaged
for us in Mary, just as we have been made in the fatherhood
of God, through Christ, the divine Son.

MARY WITHOUT CHILD

When we consider Mary apart from her thousands of
attributes, she is remarkably simple and powerful. She is no
longer a means to an end. She is no longer any of those
tremendous things that she surely was: Bride of the celestial
Bridegroom, archetype of the Church, Mother of God, New
Eve. Instead, when we consider her completely alone, Mary
is a symbol of the feminine side of God. She prays, but not

in the medieval style of abject devotion, or with eyes turned toward heaven. Instead, she stands and prays with arms wide open, looking straight ahead—a guide, rather than a

disciple. She is no longer a symbol of fine, worldly beauty, but instead, a majestic woman of deep wisdom. Ironically, when her grandeur is set aside, we can then see her wisdom more clearly.

Luther was very clear that it is wrong to regard the Virgin Mother as a divine being. He was also hesitant to use the title "Queen of Heaven" for her. Without rejecting it completely, Luther still taught: "'Queen of Heaven' . . . is a true-enough name and yet does not make her a goddess who could grant gifts or render aid, as some suppose when they pray and flee to her rather than to God. She gives nothing. God gives all."[95] But it was still true for Luther that Mary exemplified a side of holiness that makes her the unique Mother of God. She still acts as our spiritual mother.

What does it mean for us today that Mary is our mother? Feminist Catholic scholar Rosemary Radford Ruether offers an answer in her explanation of Mary as the exemplar of humankind, of the Church, of us. "Only through Mary's *fiat* was Christ born, and only with her consent was he offered up for our sins. This view suggests the importance of human consent to God's grace. God saves us only through our cooperation with his grace, not against our will."[96]

"I am black and beautiful, O daughters of Jerusalem, like the tents of Kedar, like the curtains of Solomon," says the Song of Songs, chapter one. Where does her beauty come from? What makes her shine for all generations? Modern artists and contemporary theologians alike have stirred controversies with their portrayals of Mary as a real person: a poor peasant, probably fighting to scratch out a living, an unwed mother, an outcast to those who knew her. I suppose that there is something compelling about these portraits in that they show Mary to be a woman like us, and they show that God comes to everyone regardless of status, power, wealth, or physical beauty. But, on the other hand, there is no reason to doubt that Mary was beautiful. She shone.

In the first part of this book we looked at those who once praised Mary for her delicacy, refinement, and comeliness. These ideas sprang from the minds of men who were seeking the ideal woman of beauty to be the mother of their savior. They were ways of making Mary into the perfect mother, the ideal wife. In contrast, there are images of Mary that show her to be beautiful because she shines from within. Her confidence, her faith, her ability to combine the divine and human in her own willing for the future, allow her to glow with a beauty that is a part of grace. She is a feminine face of God.

In Sue Monk Kidd's *The Secret Life of Bees*, the character August says to the narrator, Lilly: "You have a mother inside yourself. We all do. Even if we already have a mother, we still have to find this part of ourselves inside."[97] August (and Kidd) are reflecting on their experiences of visiting a statue of the Black Madonna, one of the principal characters in the novel. In a sort of conclusion to these notions, August reflects, "She is a muscle of love, this Mary." That is the image of her that seems to fit the best.

Strange Heaven

THE APOSTLE PAUL MADE ONLY ONE COMMENT about her, and it was really a statement about Jesus. He said that Christ was "born of a woman" (Galatians 4:4). In other words, God is made of the same stuff that we are made of. How strange is that? Have you looked at yourself lately?

Not only is Mary the chief connection we have to Christ, she is his throne—*Sedes Sapientiae*, "Throne of Wisdom," as it was said during the Middle Ages.

Strange Heaven

When the magi arrived on the Epiphany, Jesus could have sat alone, meeting them on his own terms, a child facing the wisdom of the world. But, why isn't he pictured that way, by the great artists who have taken this subject up? Mary was his birth mother, but she was also his primary companion. We have no biblical stories about Jesus with his playgroup. Mary was his playmate, his teacher, his comforter. She can be ours, too.

Saints are not only biblical and historical figures from the past that are long gone; they are alive and waiting for us, cheering us on. They are that marvelous "cloud of witnesses" spoken of in the New Testament, but even more than that, they are not just watching; they are listening and even accompanying us on the way. This doesn't mean that we try and reproduce their lives in our own; we have a deeper work to do. Contemporary Catholic scholar Elizabeth A. Johnson writes eloquently about Mary:

> Walking by faith, not by sight, she composes her life as a friend of God and a prophet, one who actively partners the divine work of repairing the world. . . . [T]he circumstances of her actual life can never be repeated. But the style and spirit of her responses reverberate through the centuries to encourage the practice of discipleship in today's different cultural contexts. This is more than giving example. In solidarity with her . . . contemporary people experience the impetus to face up to their own encounters with the Spirit and go forward with the best of their faithful wits.[98]

We should do away with the modern invention—since the Reformation and then the Enlightenment—that we stand before God alone and face the Last Judgment alone, and that we must face up to obedience and fidelity alone before God. Kierkegaard emphasized this side of faith and talked at length about "the individual" who is the only reality of faith. I don't think so. There are saints past and present who are in your corner, rooting for you. Praying for each other and living in community are two realities in Christian faith that are not bound by space and time.

Mary doesn't want to be a theological argument. She's not a sticking point. She is the Mother of God and a mother for all of us.

Each of us had a mother, and none of our ancestors have ever done without one. We are attached to our mothers in the womb, and we become unattached to them as soon as we enter the world. (Even though we sometimes wish that we could attach ourselves, again!) We enter the world ready to see, want, seek, and recognize our mothers. In the West, at least, Eve and Mary are the primary symbols of that sort of motherhood. Other images sometimes replace traditional mothers in the human imagination: We have seen eras, for instance, when nation and country becomes like mother. Also, we often feel the embrace of "mother" on oceans, in forests, and perhaps, cathedrals. Christianity has focused us on two, primary mothers; Eve's somehow failed, and Mary's represents a restoration, a kind of wholeness.

We should conclude almost where we began, where this all began—at the Annunciation to Mary. This most remarkable event in history is also the most painted one. There are more paintings of the Annunciation than of any other scene in history. And it causes us to reflect: Where does salvation begin and where does it end? Perhaps the answer is that it doesn't. We are involved in a continuing circle of connections to heaven and earth that began somewhere between the beginning of time, the Incarnation, the Annunciation, and the Cross. And it never really ends. As Rowan Williams explains about icons that picture Mary pointing to Jesus and Jesus looking back at her: "So she looks at us, urging us by her gesture *not* to keep our eyes on her face but to follow the hand that points to Jesus; he looks at her, drawing us back to her face; and the face that is the object of Christ's loving gaze is precisely the face that looks not to him but to us, eager for our looking to be turned, converted, to *him*. The path is one where everything is in movement."[99]

The Annunciation is God at home in us, in the very stuff of us. It is God's surprising insistence that we are where redemption for the world begins. If the Cross is the accomplishment of salvation, the birth of God in Mary is its consummation. Beginning at the Annunciation, Mary slowly came to understand the strange mystery inside of her, and then all around her. She is the chief symbol of his humanity, and her strange heaven is what is possible in all of us.

Acknowledgments

MANY THANKS GO TO PATRICIA NAKAMURA, MY THOUGHTFUL and wise editor. Many thanks also to the College of Preachers at The National Cathedral in Washington, D.C., for a quiet weekend of study in the autumn of 2004. And thanks to my wife and partner, Danelle, for her infinite patience and wisdom over the last eighteen months.

Most of the illustrations that appear throughout this book come from the classic volume *Legends of the Madonna as Represented in the Fine Arts,* by the nine-teenth-century art historian and critic Anna Brownell Jameson (first edition 1852). We have taken these illustra tions from a 1907 reprint of the second edition for these fine, simple representations of the Virgin.

The twentieth-century philosopher Ludwig Wittgenstein once commented that the purpose of using Scripture must be very much like using a list for groceries. Once you have gotten everything, you toss the list away. My hope is that this book—although full of facts, history, and opinion—will have this sort of practical effect for those who seek a deeper understanding and relationship with Mary.

Strange Heaven is dedicated to my friend and teacher, M. Basil Pennington, OCSO, who died on June 3, 2005. The lines quoted above on the dedication page are from an ancient chant known as "The Commemoration of the Blessed Virgin Mary." We sang those words before the final blessing at Dom Basil's funeral.

The Three Great Canticles from Luke's Gospel

THE MAGNIFICAT, A SONG OF MARY

This is the longest speech we have from Mary. It is her great song.

> My soul magnifies the Lord, and my spirit
>   rejoices in God my Savior,
> for he has looked with favor on the lowliness
>   of his servant.
> Surely, from now on all generations will call me
>   blessed;
> for the Mighty One has done great things for me,
> and holy is his name.
> His mercy is for those who fear him from
>   generation to generation.
> He has shown strength with his arm;
> he has scattered the proud in the thoughts of their
> hearts.
> He has brought down the powerful from their
>   thrones,
> and lifted up the lowly;
> he has filled the hungry with good things,
> and sent the rich away empty.
> He has helped his servant Israel, in remembrance
>   of his mercy,

according to the promise he made to our ancestors,
to Abraham and to his descendents forever.
  —Luke 1:46–55

THE BENEDICTUS, A SONG OF ZACHARIAH

Zachariah, the husband of Elizabeth and father of John
the Baptist, was struck dumb by the angel Gabriel for failing to
have faith. When he finally recovered his voice, he sang to
God.

Blessed be the Lord God of Israel,
for he has looked favorably on his people and
    redeemed them.
He has raised up a mighty savior for us
in the house of his servant David,
as he spoke through the mouth of his holy
    prophets from of old,
that we would be saved from our enemies
and from the hand of all who hate us.
Thus he has shown the mercy promised to our
    ancestors,
and has remembered his holy covenant,
the oath that he swore to our ancestor Abraham,
to grant us that we, being rescued from the hands
    of our enemies,
might serve him without fear,
in holiness and righteousness before him all our
    days.
And you, child, will be called the prophet of the
    Most High;
for you will go before the Lord to prepare his
    ways,
to give knowledge of salvation to his people by

the forgiveness of their sins.
By the tender mercy of our God,
the dawn from on high will break upon us,
to give light to those who sit in darkness and in
the shadow of death,
to guide our feet into the way of peace.
—Luke 1:68–79

THE NUNC DIMITTIS, A SONG OF SIMEON

One of the most popular, if not the most popular,
hymn/prayer sung at compline services throughout the
Christian world since the earliest days of formalized liturgy.

Master, now you are dismissing your servant in
peace,
according to your word;
for my eyes have seen your salvation,
which you have prepared in the presence of all
peoples,
a light for revelation to the Gentiles
and for glory to your people Israel.
—Luke 2:29–32

A Basic Chronology for Understanding Mary

Many of these dates are only approximate. They represent the best estimates of scholars today.

900 BC	The Song of Hannah (1 Samuel 2:1–10)
800 BC	Psalms of David
700 BC	Hebrew prophet Isaiah foretells of a virgin who will bear a child (Isaiah 7:14)
63 BC	The Romans take control of Jerusalem and the provinces of Palestine
4 BC	Herod the Great, Roman ruler of Palestine, dies [100]
AD 5	The Annunciation and Mary's Magnificat (Luke 1:46–55)
6	The Nativity of Our Lord
39	Passion of Christ. Mary goes to Ephesus with St. John?
60–69	Dormition and Assumption of Mary
65	Gospel of Mark written
100	Last of canonical Gospels (John) written; Gospel of Thomas written
325	First Churchwide Council of Nicaea. New Testament canon is set.
430	St. Augustine of Hippo dies

Appendix B

431	Church Council of Ephesus. *Theotokos* affirmed.
632	Prophet Muhammad dies
750–850	*The Gospel of the Birth of Mary* compiled
1095	Pope Urban II preaches the First Crusade
1150	Peter Lombard publishes *The Sentences*, which denies the Immaculate Conception
1153	St. Bernard of Clairvaux dies
1260	Jacobus de Voragine compiles *The Golden Legend*. It was first published in English by Caxton's press, after his death, in 1493.
Early 1300s	*Angelus* prayer (anonymous)
1321	Dante Alighieri dies
1400	Geoffrey Chaucer dies
	Julian of Norwich writes her *Showings*
1470s	Rosary use becomes widespread in the West
1490s	Popular devotion books first printed and made widely available
1505	Young Martin Luther cries out in terror, "St. Anne help me! I will become a monk."
1517	Luther nails his *Ninety-five Theses* on the door of the Wittenberg church
1522	The conversion of St. Ignatius of Loyola
1525	William Tyndale's English New Testament
1531	Juan Diego sees the Virgin of Guadalupe, Mexico
1534	Luther's vernacular German Bible first published
1536	Erasmus dies
1545–63	The Counter Reformation's Council of Trent

Strange Heaven

1716	St. Louis-Marie de Montfort dies
1842	Montfort's *True Devotion to Mary* first published
1858	Bernadette sees the Virgin at Lourdes, France
1859	Charles Darwin publishes *The Origin of Species*
1910	The Virgin of Guadalupe declared the patroness of the Americas
1950	Pope Pius XII proclaims the dogma of the Assumption of Mary
1954	Pope Pius XII proclaims Mary the Queen of Heaven
1963–5	The Second Vatican Council
1981	Pope John Paul II shot in Rome. He later explains that Our Lady of Fatima changed the path of the bullet in order to save his life.
2005	Pope John Paul II dies. His reported last words were spoken in Latin: *Totus tuus*, "totally yours," to the Virgin Mary.

APPENDIX C

Five Legends of the Virgin Mary from the Middle Ages

The first four of these popular stories are taken from Jacobus de Voragine's *The Golden Legend*. The fifth legend can also be traced back to the later Middle Ages, and was repeated in various forms in chronicles written during the Catholic Counter Reformation as a tool for recruiting members to one of the religious orders. All are re-told by the author.

The Virgin Mary's Birthday

For many centuries after the Virgin Mary's birth, we did not know the day of her blessed and miraculous birth. It was a lonely, devoted man of quiet solitude and prayer to whom the day was first revealed.

We do not know his name, but this holy man was deep in prayer each day to the Virgin. Day after day he would sit diligently and faithfully in quiet contemplation. Very little changed for this holy man from one week to the next, or from one year to the next.

But one day, the man realized as he was praying that he heard the sound of choirs of angels chanting the psalms. It was a sound of such beauty and joy that he reveled in it all the day long. The angels joined him as he prayed the Divine Office, and when he went to bed that evening (although he slept very little), the sound of their singing still hummed in his ears. But when he woke up the next day, and he put himself back to prayer, the lovely chanting was gone. Still, he prayed as he always had prayed before.

A year passed, and the holy man once again heard those angelic voices singing the Psalms of David. The man at once realized that the day was the eighth of September and, after a moment of reflection, that it was the previous year on that very same day that he first had heard the beautiful singing of angels while he prayed. So, he prayed to God for an answer: Why was he hearing these voices once each year? The answer came quickly: "This is the day that the blessed Mary was born," God said.

A Devoted Knight

There once was a knight who was fearless in combat and fervently devoted to the Blessed Virgin Mary. When he fought, he fought as if he had Mary at his side; and he was always victorious. One day, while on his way to a tournament—where he would once again show his valor and strength—the knight came upon a monastery built in Mary's honor. He dismounted from his horse and entered the sacred place in order to hear Mass. He sat quietly, his sword at his side, and blissfully reveled in the holy words of the liturgy to the Blessed Virgin. When the liturgy was over, the knight gathered his things to leave, but then, he saw that there was another Mass for the Virgin about to begin. The devoted knight did not want to miss any Mass that was said for his patron. And so he stayed.

At the conclusion of the second Mass, the knight's mind immediately turned toward his tournament, where he would demonstrate his great prowess and give glory to Mary. But, as he was about to leave the sanctuary, yet another Mass had begun. He sat down in all reverence. This happened again and again that day, as one Mass followed quickly upon another.

Finally, the great knight rode away from the monastery and urged his horse along as fast as he could travel. He didn't know how late he would be, by the time he arrived at the tournament. But before long, the knight was met on the road by several other knights traveling in the opposite direction. They were returning home from the field after the tournament.

"Hail, good knight!" one of them called out. "You were the greatest, today," congratulated another. "The best of us all!" yelled out another.

The knight was confused, until he realized that Mary, the Queen of Heaven, had honored him for his devotion. He smiled as he turned his horse around, returning to the monastery for the night.

A Tale of Two Hostage Sons

It is a terrible thing for a wife to lose her husband away at war. How such a woman must feel, then, to see her only son leaving in armor, too! Well, there was such a woman living many years ago; her only son, her only consolation in a difficult life, went away to war and was captured by his enemies, imprisoned in chains. News of this calamity got back to the mother and she wept for three days. She was inconsolable during that time and would not eat or drink or sleep.

On the fourth day, the woman turned to the Blessed Virgin Mary. The woman was greatly devoted to the Holy Mother and she turned to her, asking her intercession for her son's freedom. She prayed in this way for three days and nights.

At the end of three days, the woman could feel that her prayers were not yet answered. She was so close with her son that she knew she would know when he was imprisoned and when he was free. She could still see him in a very dark place, bound in chains. So, the woman left her house and walked to a lonely church in her village where there was a sculpture image of Mary with the child Jesus on her lap. There, she again prayed, saying, "Blessed Virgin, I have asked you for the freedom of my only son, and so far you have not come to my aid. I speak to you, a mother who knew great sorrow, as a woman who has only known sorrow these many years. Answer me."

The woman heard and felt nothing, and so she continued: "If my only son is to be taken away from me, Blessed Virgin, then I will also take away your son!" She jumped up and snatched the statue of the Christ child from the lap of his mother, and bolted from the church. She took him home, wrapped him in swaddling clothes, and hid him in her cupboard, locking the door carefully.

The next day, as the woman's son lay in that prison, sad and alone, the Virgin Mary appeared suddenly to him. She pulled out a key and opened the door to his cell and invited him to leave, saying, "You are free, son. Now, go and tell your mother to give me back my son, as well." The young man, quite astonished, left the prison as quickly as his weak legs could carry him, and brought the message to his dear mother. She was overjoyed and embraced him with all of her heart and soul, vowing that he would not leave her side again.

The determined mother went to her cupboard and gathered up the Christ child. She unwrapped him and carried him back to the church in town. As she placed him back on the statue of his mother's arms, she said to Mary: "Thank you, dear Lady, for bringing my son home. I am glad to return yours, as well."

Appendix C

The Thief and the Hangman

There once was a thief who stole into his neighbor's homes as they slept and robbed them of their valuables. His own home was rich with silver, and candles, and religious relics from far-off pilgrimages that he had never taken. He was a small man, and very quiet in his movements, and had never before been caught.

This thief was also devoted to the Virgin Mary. He praised her for his successes, and he remembered the grace that she had shown to his own mother when she was in need, when he was just a boy. And so, this devoted thief would pray fifty *Aves* during and after his thefts, giving thanks to the Queen of Heaven. He also gave a portion of each robbery to the Blessed Virgin.

One day, the thief was leaving a house in the dead of night with armloads of fine clothing when the landowner and his servants arrived suddenly from a long journey. The house had been empty and now, suddenly, the owner was there, standing before him. The thief was captured by the lord's men. The local lords searched his house and discovered his many crimes, and the thief was quickly sentenced to be hanged.

A few days later, with all of the people in the town watching, as he stood under a large oak waiting for the noose to be fastened around his neck, the thief prayed to the Virgin: "Save me, holy Mother! I put all of my trust in you." With those last words, the hangman put the rope around the man's neck and he was raised off his feet, up into the tree.

As the thief hung from the tree, he knew that Mary was beside him, and was holding up his feet just enough so that he could not feel any pressure on his neck. He hung there quietly, and he praised Mary in his heart. He did not die, and was not even injured. After a short while,

217

the crowd grew bored and dispersed, but the thief (and Mary) remained there, hanging quietly, for three more days.

After three days had passed, the hangman walked by that place again to inspect it, in preparation for another man's sentence. He stopped to examine the thief, whose eyes were wide open and who was smiling gaily at his executioner. The hangman, anxious that he would be found out to have done a poor job of tying the noose around the thief's neck, reached for his sword to finish the man off once and for all. But as he pulled the sword from its sheath, the Virgin Mary (who was completely invisible to the hangman, for he had no faith) struck it down with a mighty blow. The sword flew from the hangman's hand and was split in two as it crashed against another oak.

The hangman immediately knelt in the dirt, crossed himself, and refused to raise his head. "Please, please," the joyful thief called out to him, "Help me down from here and I will tell you all that has happened." And so the executioner untied the thief and all was soon revealed. Both the thief and the executioner, for love of the Virgin, went off and joined a monastery, where they lived the rest of their days as brothers in service to the mother of God.

She Pleads for Us before the Judgment Seat

There was once a priest and monk named William who lived in Clairvaux. He was devout in his daily prayers, and to him were given many secrets and private revelations. One afternoon, as he stood in prayer alone in his cell, William fell into an ecstasy of mind. He was taken up to heaven in his vision where a multitude of angels was carrying a great throne and setting it down in a wide, open space. Then, William saw the most fearsome and beautiful angels carrying Christ, as the angry Judge, and placing him on top of the throne.

An archangel stood at Christ's right hand with a trumpet in his right hand. William had never felt so much fear and trembling as he did at that moment throughout all of heaven. Christ turned to the angel and said, "Sound your blast." The entire world shook and trembled at the sound of that trumpet, for its fierce bellowing was so great. Buildings collapsed, trees shook loose from their roots, and all people stopped their talking.

There was a moment of stillness after that first blast, and then Christ said to the angel, "Now, it is time to sound the second blast." At the feet of Christ the Judge were the books that repeated the deeds of all who had lived on the earth. Christ was listening to these deeds, and as he listened, he became angrier and angrier at the evil deeds done by men and women. The second trumpet blast would bring about the end of the world. All of the saints in heaven knew that it would happen this way, but they remained silent and were afraid.

Christ was in a fury. Just as he was about to seize the world as though it were a little ball in his hand, William of Clairvaux called out: "Holy Mary, succor us in our time of trial!" The Virgin Mary, our Lord's dear mother and the Mother of all Mercy, came rushing to Christ's feet. She said: "Spare them, my beloved son. Spare them once again, and this time, the [Franciscans, Dominicans, Cistercians, etc.] will recall the world to Thee."

It was at Mary's request that Christ let go of the little ball in his hand, and earthquakes and tornados burst out around the earth. But after a short time, all was safe once again.

NOTES

1   G. G. Coulton, *Life in the Middle Ages, Vol. IV,* (New York: Macmillan, 1935), 169. Translated quotes from Coulton's book have been occasionally updated according to modern spelling and usage.

2   Lesley Hazleton, *Mary: A Flesh-and-Blood Biography of the Virgin Mother* (New York: Bloomsbury, 2004), 1.

3   Pope John Paul II quote taken from John L. Allen's weekly column, "The Word from Rome," *National Catholic Reporter*, August 27, 2004.

4   Andrew Greeley, *The Catholic Imagination* (Berkeley: Univ. of California Press, 2001), 1.

5   Rowan Williams, *Ponder These Things: Praying with Icons of the Virgin* (Brewster, MA: Paraclete Press, 2006), xv.

6   Mark 6:3, John 16:28, and Hebrews 7:3.

7   Bernard of Clairvaux, *Song of Songs III*, trans. by Kilian Walsh and Irene M. Edmonds (Kalamazoo, MI: Cistercian Publications, 1979); from Sermon 54, 69-70.

8   From her poem "Why I Love You, O Mary!" in *The Poetry of Saint Thérèse of Lisieux*, trans. by Donald Kinney, OCD (Washington, D.C.: ICS Publications, 1996), 217.

9   Quoted in Jaroslav Pelikan, *Mary through the Centuries: Her Place in the History of Culture* (New Haven: Yale University Press, 1996), 156-7.

10 Cheryl A. Kirk-Duggan, "Proud Mary: Contextual Constructions of a Divine Diva," in *Blessed One: Protestant Perspectives on Mary*, eds. Beverly Roberts Gaventa and Cynthia L. Rigby (Louisville: Westminster John Knox Press, 2002), 71-2.

11 Augustine, *The City of God*, Book XIV, chapter xvi. When I quote from *The City of God*, I am using the classic translation of John Healey but with small changes for contemporary use and gender-inclusiveness.

12 J. N. D. Kelly, *Jerome: His Life, Writings, and Controversies* (New York: Harper & Row, 1975), 189.

13 Hildegard of Bingen, as quoted in Rosemary Radford Ruether's *Goddesses and the Divine Feminine: A Western Religious History* (Berkeley: University of California Press, 2005), 172.

14 Epiphanius, quoted in *Spiritual Writings on Mary: Annotated & Explained*, ed. by Mary Ford-Grabowsky (Woodstock, VT: SkyLight Paths Publishing, 2005), 39.

15 Chapter 13. As noted in the discussion of this text in chapter three, all quotes are taken from the translation of The Gnostic Society Library online version, www.gnosis.org.

16 From "The Life of St. Christine the Astonishing," trans. by Elizabeth Spearing, in *Medieval Writings on Female Spirituality*, ed. Elizabeth Spearing (New York: Penguin, 2002), 77.

17 *The Revelations of Mechthild of Magdeburg, or The Flowing Light of the Godhead*, trans. Lucy Menzies (New York: Longmans, Green and Co., 1953), 13.

18 Both antiphons are taken from the translation found in *Secrets of God: Writings of Hildegard of Bingen* (Boston: Shambhala Publications, 1996), 137, 123.

19 Mary Daly, *Webster's First New Intergalactic Wickedary of the English Language* (Boston: Beacon Press, 1987), 176.

20 From *The Mary Book*, ed. F. J. Sheed (New York: Sheed & Ward, 1951), 15-16.

21 All of these preceding Latin translations are quoted from *English Religious Lyrics in the Middle Ages*, by Rosemary Woolf (Oxford: Oxford University Press, 1968), 115-16.

Notes

22 Jacobus de Voragine, *The Golden Legend: Readings on the Saints*, trans. William Granger Ryan (Princeton, NJ: Princeton University Press, 1993), Vol. 2, 119. All quotations from this text will be taken from this edition.

23 *The Revelations of Mechthild of Magdeburg, or The Flowing Light of the Godhead*, trans. Menzies, 13.

24 This phrase is Ingrid Rowland's characterization of Bernardino's 1427 sermon, taken from "What the Frescoes Said," by Ingrid Rowland, *The New York Review of Books*, October 20, 2005, 37.

25 Elizabeth A. Johnson, *Dangerous Memories: A Mosaic of Mary in Scripture* (New York: Continuum, 2004), 153.

26 *The Poetry of Saint Thérèse of Lisieux*, trans. by Donald Kinney, OCD (Washington, D.C.: ICS Publications, 1996), 220.

27 Albert Schweitzer, *The Mysticism of Paul the Apostle* (London: Adam and Charles Black, 1953), 123–5.

28 All quotes from *The Gospel of the Birth of Mary*, or *The Gospel of Pseudo-Matthew*, are taken from the translation of The Gnostic Society Library online: www.gnosis.org.

29 Jalal ad-Din Rumi, *Tales from the Masnavi*, trans. A. J. Arberry (London: George Allen & Unwin Ltd., 1961), 267.

30 Jalal ad-Din Rumi from the *Masnavi*, quoted in *Jesus in the Eyes of the Sufis*, by Javad Nurbakhsh (London: Khaniqahi-Nimatullahi Publications, 1983), 28-9.

31 Virginia Nixon, *Mary's Mother: Saint Anne in Late Medieval Europe* (University Park, PA: The Pennsylvania State University Press, 2004), 16.

32 Sally Cunneen, *In Search of Mary: The Woman and the Symbol* (New York: Ballantine Books, 1996), 169.

33 This classic text is now in the public domain, but all quotes that follow are taken from the edition published in London by Burns & Oates, 1955.

34 St. Bridget of Sweden, from *Medieval Writings on Female Spirituality*, ed. from Spearing, 150-1.

35 Translation of Abraham Coles, with changes by the author.

36 Kathleen Norris, foreword to *Blessed One: Protestant Perspectives on Mary*, eds. Beverly Roberts Gaventa and Cynthia L. Rigby (Louisville: Westminster John Knox Press, 2002), xii.

37 Phoebe Griswold, "An Ecumenical Mary / Tracking Mary," a lecture delivered at Fordham University in October, 2004, and published in the online journal of the Ecumenical Society of the Blessed Virgin Mary—United States, www.msa62.tripod.com/esbvm/.

38 *Dogmatic Constitution on the Church, Lumen Gentium*, solemnly promulgated by His Holiness Pope Paul VI on November 21, 1964. See the Catholic Information Network website, www.cin.org, for the full document.

39 Williams, *Ponder These Things: Praying with Icons of the Virgin*, xiv.

40 Mary Lee Nolan and Sidney Nolan, *Christian Pilgrimage in Modern Western Europe* (Chapel Hill: University of North Carolina Press, 1989), 9.

41 Quoted in Pelikan, *Mary through the Centuries: Her Place in the History of Culture*, 178-9.

42 Chris Tisch, "Virgin Mary vandal receives light sentence, prayers," *St. Petersburg Times*, July 13, 2004.

43 "Virgin Mary image returns," by Patrick Rucker and Nancy Ryan, *Chicago Tribune*, May 6, 2005.

44 "Some see Virgin Mary in underpass stain," CNN.com, April 20, 2005; and "Police: Man defaced Virgin Mary image," CNN.com, May 6, 2005.

45 John Cornwell makes this point in his article "He Believed in Miracles," *Vanity Fair*, June 2005, 116–124.

46 One caveat about Fatima: The village is named for a princess who was, in turn, named after the daughter of the Prophet Muhammad. This all happened in the days when the Moors (followers of Muhammad) occupied Portugal. Muhammad

Notes

once said of his daughter, Fatima: "She has the highest place in heaven after the Virgin Mary." It is remarkable how many Muslims make pilgrimages to Our Lady of Fatima's shrine each year. It is a place that brings Christians and Muslims together in ways that are seemingly impossible today in the shared holy places of Jerusalem.

47 Quoted in Diana Norman, *Siena and the Virgin: Art and Politics in a Late Medieval City State* (New Haven: Yale University Press, 1999), 3.

48 Wayne Weible, *A Child Shall Lead Them: Stories of Transformed Young Lives in Medjugorje* (Brewster, MA: Paraclete Press, 2005), xii.

49 Sue Monk Kidd, *The Secret Life of Bees* (New York, Penguin, 2002).

50 Augusta T. Drane, *A History of St. Dominic* (London: Longmans Green, 1891), 22.

51 Coulton, *Life in the Middle Ages, Vol. IV*, 322.

52 Sometime around the fifteenth century, perhaps through the leadership of St. Bernardino of Siena, the Franciscans developed a specifically Marian rosary. This is called the "Seven Joys," or the Franciscan Crown, or the Seraphic Rosary, and it focuses the prayerful on remembering seven joyful episodes in the life of Mary. Most of these are found in the traditional rosary, but one is new: The Annunciation, The Visitation, The Nativity, The Adoration of the Magi, Jesus in the Temple, Christ's Resurrection, and Mary's Assumption.

53 Kidd, *The Secret Life of Bees*.

54 Megan McKenna, *Praying the Rosary: A Complete Guide to the World's Most Popular Form of Prayer* (New York: Doubleday, 2004), 41-2.

55 See the literal, but beautiful, translation of "Why I Love You, O Mary!" in *The Poetry of Saint Thérèse of Lisieux*, trans. Kinney, OCD, 215–220.

56 Pope John XXIII, *Journal of a Soul*, trans. Dorothy White

(New York: McGraw-Hill, 1965), 56.

57 Quoted in "The Bedside: Pope's Visitors Saw Serenity in Final Hours," by Elaine Sciolino and Daniel J. Wakin. *The New York Times*, page A12, April 4, 2005.

58 Bishop Kallistos Ware, *The Orthodox Way* (Crestwood, NY: St. Vladamir's Seminary Press, 2002), 76-77.

59 From *Lumen Gentium*, par. 62.

60 Coulton, *Life in the Middle Ages, Vol. I*, 234.

61 Leonardo Boff, *The Maternal Face of God: The Feminine and Its Religious Expressions* (Maryknoll, NY: Orbis Books, 1987), 130.

62 Pope John XXIII, *Journal of a Soul*, trans. White, 314.

63 Coulton, *Life in the Middle Ages, Vol. II*, 138-40.

64 John of Damascus, from "On the Falling Asleep of the Mother of God," in *Mary in the Documents of the Church*, ed. by Paul F. Palmer (Westminster, MD: Newman Press, 1952), 60.

65 Louis-Marie Grignion de Montfort, quoted in *Perfect Fools: Folly for Christ's Sake in Catholic and Orthodox Spirituality*, by John Saward, trans. Saward (New York: Oxford University Press, 1980), 187.

66 "Women of the Bible: Provocative New Insights," *U.S. News and World Report*, December 2005, 65.

67 *The Odes of Solomon: The Syriac Texts*, ed. and trans. James H. Charlesworth (Missoula, MT: Scholars Press, 1977), 82-3, 124.

68 *The Revelations of Mechthild of Magdeburg, or The Flowing Light of the Godhead*, trans. Menzies, 14.

69 Bernard of Clairvaux, *Song of Songs I*, trans. by Kilian Walsh (Kalamazoo, MI: Cistercian Publications, 1981) from Sermon 9; 55, 58.

70 *Five Centuries of Religion, Volume I* (Cambridge: Cambridge University Press, 1929), 151.

71 *The Oxford Book of Welsh Verse in English*, ed. Gwyn Jones (New York: Oxford University Press, 1977), 48.

Notes

72 Coulton, *Life in the Middle Ages, Vol. IV,* 258.

73 Bernard of Clairvaux, *Song of Songs I,* trans. Kilian Walsh (Kalamazoo, MI: Cistercian Publications, 1981); from Sermon 10; 62-3.

74 S.H. Steinberg, *Five Hundred Years of Printing* (Baltimore: Penguin Books, 1966), 143-4.

75 Translation by Virginia Nixon, in *Mary's Mother: Saint Anne in Late Medieval Europe,* by Virginia Nixon (University Park, PA: The Pennsylvania State University Press, 2004), 43.

76 Martin Luther, *Luther's Works, Volume 54,* general editor Helmut T. Lehmann (Philadelphia: Fortress Press, 1967), 84.

77 Martin Luther, *Luther's Works, Volume 22,* edited by Jaroslav Pelikan (St. Louis: Concordia Publishing House, 1957), 377. For the text of Bernard's "Sermon on the Octave of the Assumption of the Blessed Virgin Mary" see Giovanni Miegge's *The Virgin Mary: The Roman Catholic Marian Doctrine* (London: Lutterworth Press, 1955).

78 Bernard of Clairvaux, *Song of Songs IV,* trans. Irene Edmonds (Kalamazoo, MI: Cistercian Publications, 1980); from Sermon 73; 78.

79 *The Collected Works of St. John of the Cross,* trans. by Kieran Kavanaugh, OCD, and Otilio Rodriguez, OCD (Washington, D.C.: Institute of Carmelite Studies, 1991), 73.

80 Martin Luther, from his "Sermon on the Nativity," in *Here I Stand: A Life of Martin Luther,* by Roland H. Bainton (New York: Abingdon Press, 1950), 354.

81 Bainton, *Here I Stand: A Life of Martin Luther,* 21.

82 Martin Luther in a letter to Melanchthon, in *Luther's Works, Volume 21,* edited by Jaroslav Pelikan (St. Louis: Concordia Publishing House, 1956), xviii.

83 Martin Luther, from "The Magnificat," translated by A. T. W. Steinhaeuser, in *Luther's Works, Volume 21,* 314.

84 Ibid., 321.

85 Martin Luther, *Luther's Works, Volume 21,* 326.

86 Ibid., 322. Two slight word changes have been made to bring the translation to present English usage.

87 Martin Luther, from his "Sermon on the Nativity," in *Here I Stand: A Life of Martin Luther*, Bainton 354-55.

88 Martin Luther, from "The Magnificat," 322-23.

89 Martin Luther, from "The Magnificat," 329.

90 Soren Kierkegaard, *Training in Christianity*, trans. Walter Lowrie (Princeton: Princeton University Press, 1944), 108.

91 Frederick William Faber, preface to *True Devotion to the Blessed Virgin Mary*, by St. Louis Mary de Montfort, trans. Frederick William Faber (Bay Shore, New York: The Montfort Fathers' Publications, 1950), xi-xii.

92 Pope John XXIII, *Journal of a Soul*, trans. White, 315.

93 *True Devotion to the Blessed Virgin Mary*, trans. Faber, pars. 29 and 31.

94 Ibid., pars. 16 and 18.

95 Martin Luther, from "The Magnificat," 327-28.

96 Rosemary Radford Ruether, *Goddesses and the Divine Feminine: A Western Religious History* (Berkeley: University of California Press, 2005), 166.

97 Kidd, *The Secret Life of Bees*.

98 Elizabeth A. Johnson, *Truly Our Sister: A Theology of Mary in the Communion of Saints* (New York: Continuum, 2003), 209.

99 Williams, *Ponder These Things*, 9-10.

100 Many scholars today believe that the story found only in Matthew's Gospel of the Massacre of the Innocents by Herod is a myth allegedly fulfilling a prophecy by Jeremiah and mirroring history's judgment of the great but evil potentate Herod. See Michael Grant, *Jesus: An Historian's Review of the Gospels*; New York: Scribner's, 1977; 71. In other words, the implication is that Herod the Great was no longer ruler of Palestine at the time of Christ's birth.

229

Index

Index

About Paraclete Press

Who We Are

Paraclete Press is an ecumenical publisher of books and recordings on Christian spirituality. Our publishing represents a full expression of Christian belief and practice—from Catholic to Evangelical, from Protestant to Orthodox.

Paraclete Press is the publishing arm of the Community of Jesus, an ecumenical monastic community in the Benedictine tradition. As such, we are uniquely positioned in the marketplace without connection to a large corporation and with informal relationships to many branches and denominations of faith.

We like it best when people buy our books from booksellers, our partners in successfully reaching as wide an audience as possible.

What We Are Doing

Paraclete Press publishes books that show the richness and depth of what it means to be Christian. Although Benedictine spirituality is at the heart of all that we do, we publish books that reflect the Christian experience across many cultures, time periods, and houses of worship.

We publish books that nourish the vibrant life of the church and its people—books about spiritual practice, formation, history, ideas, and customs.

We have several different series of books within Paraclete Press, including the bestselling *Living Library* series of modernized classic texts; *A Voice from the Monastery*—giving voice to men and women monastics about what it means to live a spiritual life today; award winning literary faith fiction; and books that explore Judaism and Islam and discover how these faiths inform Christian thought and practice.

Recordings

From Gregorian chant to contemporary American choral works, our music recordings celebrate the richness of sacred choral music through the centuries. Paraclete is proud to distribute the recordings of the internationally acclaimed choir Gloriæ Dei Cantores, who have been praised for their "rapt and fathomless spiritual intensity" by *American Record Guide,* and the Gloriæ Dei Cantores Schola, which specializes in the study and performance of Gregorian chant. Paraclete is also the exclusive North American distributor of the Monastic Choir of St. Peter's Abbey in Solesmes, France, long considered to be a leading authority on Gregorian chant performance.

Learn more about us at our Web site:
www.paracletepress.com, or call us toll-free at
1-800-451-5006.

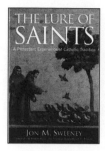

The Lure of Saints
A Protestant Experience of Catholic Tradition
Jon M. Sweeney
240 pages
Hardcover: $21.95; ISBN: 1-55725-419-2
Trade Paper: $15.95; ISBN: 1-55725-506-7

Explore how these exemplary men and women—the saints—have impacted both the Church and the world. This guide includes profiles of ancient, medieval, and modern figures, Eastern and Western, the sublime and the unusual. Also included are the personal reflections of other religious teachers and writers on how they relate to one or more of the saints in everyday life.

> "These profiles of holy men and women might inspire you to take more seriously your own calling and aspiration to live as a saint today." -*Spirituality and Health*

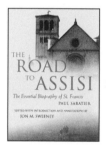

The Road to Assisi
The Essential Biography of St. Francis
Paul Sabatier
Edited with Introduction and annotations by Jon M. Sweeney
204 pages
Trade Paper: $14.95; 1-55725-401-X

A Selection of
Book of the Month Club • History Book Club
Crossings Book Club • The Literary Guild

In his 1894 biography of St. Francis, Paul Sabatier portrayed a fully human Francis, with insecurities and fear, but also a gentle mystic and passionate reformer who desired to live as Jesus taught His disciples. This modern edition of Sabatier's biography is supplemented with helpful notes, sidebars, and maps, and with the insights of scholars and writers from Dante to Umberto Eco.

Available from most bookstores or through Paraclete Press:
www.paracletepress.com • 1-800-451-5006.
Try your local bookstore first.